A RULE FOR THE CLERGY

MEDITATIONS ON ORDAINED PASTORAL MINISTRY

Fr Gerard Bogan

*All books are published
thanks to the generosity of the supporters
of the Catholic Truth Society*

Images: Cover: *Christ Pantocrator*, Inhouse CTS illustration, 2019. **Page 3:** *Crucifix*, Master of the Orcagnesque Misericordia. Gift of Samuel H. Kress, 1927, The Metropolitan Museum of Art, Washington. **Page 6:** *The Last Supper*, Ugolino da Siena. Robert Lehman Collection, 1975, The Metropolitan Museum of Art, Washington. **Page 99:** *The Descent of the Holy Spirit*, 1594-95, Rottenhammer, Hans I or Johann (1564-1625) / Gemaeldegalerie Alte Meister, Kassel, Germany / © Museumslandschaft Hessen Kassel / Ute Brunzel / Bridgeman Images. **Page 121:** *Madonna and Child*. Jorisvo / Shutterstock.com.

All biblical quotations are taken from *The Jerusalem Bible* (London: DLT, 1966).

ISBN 978 1 78469 607 8

CONTENTS

Foreword

We are bishops, priests and deacons of the universal Church. Although this may sound obvious, it is easy for us to be so consumed by our everyday responsibilities that we can forget we are part of something larger than our own situation. Personal discipline is one of the ways in which we respond to our pastoral concerns and at the same time persevere in our search for God. This is part of the function of a Rule in the religious life. *A Rule for the Clergy* offers an approach which is both disciplined and joyful.

When Fr Gerard Bogan told me that he was writing some reflections on the ministry of bishops, priests and deacons, I was interested but not surprised. His booklet, *A–Z of Spiritual Living*, published by The Catholic Truth Society, has sold well. He is the editor of *Lectio* which is a bi-annual magazine covering spiritual and general ecclesial issues. He also writes regularly for his parishioners. So, it was no surprise to me that he was preparing something else. I am happy to endorse this new work. May the Holy Spirit inspire us in our pastoral ministry.

✠ Joseph Toal
Bishop of Motherwell

Preface

The original idea for this book was to provide for priests and deacons involved in parish work a Rule similar to the type of Rule which has been written at various times for monastics. The obvious Rule that comes to mind is the Rule of St Benedict, and perhaps its forerunner the Rule of the Master. There are also others, notably the Rule of St Basil and the Rule of St Augustine. Less well known are the Rule of Tallaght, the Rule of Ailbe, the Rule of Comghall, the Rule of Colmcille, the Rule of Ciarán, and others. These were all written for specific situations – situations which are not those of diocesan priests. In addition to offering encouragement and advice for the community in question, they also dealt with some matters which would be important for community cohesion. In recent times a number of people have found that the Rule of St Benedict can be adapted to the lives of lay people, both in their homes and at their work. This is valuable because it helps people see that discipline is necessary for the living of the Christian life. It is discipline that gives us the support we require when many demands draw us in different directions and seek to bring chaos into our lives. It is also discipline that enables us to live an integrated life – we cannot have a 'spiritual' life which is separate from our home life or our work life.

An adaptation, however, will always be that. The Brothers of Taizé have recently published their *Rule of*

Taizé. It is interesting to note that when Brother Roger first published it, it was not called a Rule, but a Parable of Community. What was interesting was that it was not the prescriptive document that other Rules tended to be. Instead, it sought to be encouragement for the Brothers in their search for God as part of a community of faith. This gave me the idea that maybe it would be useful to have such a type of document for diocesan priests. It has also been written for deacons. Many of the sections appear only to refer to priests. This is simply because not so much has yet been written in relation to deacons; so, what has been written here about priests applies, mostly, to deacons too. And what applies to priests and deacons also applies to bishops.

Therefore, what follows in this Rule does not seek to be prescriptive, nor is it attempting to present the 'best' or only way to express such matters. It is one way. It is no more than a fraternal gift from one brother to his brothers.

ACTION AND CONTEMPLATION

…when you see these things happening: know that the kingdom of God is near. (Lk 21:31)

In the middle of our many parish activities are we able to give ourselves, and the situations in which we find ourselves, over to contemplation? This is not the same as living contemplatively. Contemplativeness is not exactly the same as contemplation, nor is contemplation able to be defined as some deep form of pious or reflective thinking. To consider contemplation in this way would allow it to be not much more than a trendy way of talking about prayer. Moreover, it would encourage an esoteric approach to prayer which would separate our prayer from our ministerial activities; it would make a division between our search for God and our caring for our parishioners. This would be false. When we try to keep in mind that contemplation is living and moving in God's presence, then we can be aware of God's presence in the middle of our work with our parishioners, or at the centre of our personal search. However, it may be helpful to avoid the obvious, maybe now hackneyed, phrase *laborare est orare*. Too often it can be understood almost in terms of work substituting prayer, rather than being prayer. Although this may be an overly precise distinction, it still presents a challenge to us to increase our awareness of being in God's presence in all circumstances.

Giving ourselves, or the situations in which we find ourselves, over to contemplation is not always easy. It may be challenging. It demands that we keep ourselves open to God's purposes, even if we cannot see the way ahead. It demands a simple trust in God's presence. It demands that we eschew any trace of cynicism and remain alive to the ideal of the Gospel.

> All our contemplation is a sharing in Christ's contemplation of his heavenly Father. All our action is valid only if it be a prolongation of the Incarnate Word, and, through him, by the Father. In a word, the active and contemplative lives are simply two aspects of the divine life which Christ lives in his members, by the action of his Holy Spirit.
>
> THOMAS MERTON [1]

ADMINISTRATION AND FINANCE

Leave the dead to bury their dead; your duty is to go and spread the news of the kingdom of God. (Lk 9:60)

Many priests will say that administration and finance is one of the areas of their lives that they could gladly do without. The argument is usually one which expresses that we were ordained to proclaim the Gospel, celebrate the sacraments and minister to God's people, not to be caught up in administrative matters. Into this area also comes the tasks involved with building and maintenance. Some find this a job they are happy to do; others feel that it is a bind upon them. How come there is so much admin? There seems to be more and more all the time. These sentiments have been echoed by many. Perhaps, however, it would be useful to remember that such matters always existed. The difference is that there are fewer priests now than in the recent past. When there were more priests the curates could divide the pastoral activities and the parish priest could attend to finance.

Maybe we have not adapted to the new situation. Might it be that we actually like being in control of such things? Moreover, there is a danger in a too-easy acceptance of the building concerns which might be easier than the demands of an often challenging pastoral ministry. Some priests have tried to free themselves from some of this burden by employing on a part-time basis someone to attend to financial concerns. Indeed, some have collaborated with other priests in sharing the same financial people. This is surely a good response to the current situation. But could we go further? Might it be possible for us to discover ways in which parish priests would not need to concern themselves with anything to do with maintenance and repairs? Would we be able to see administration as a necessary element of parish life? Would we then find it possible to give it over to suitably qualified lay people?

> These days we tend to see spirit and structures as
> being in opposition to each other. The challenge
> is to create structures which serve the spirit and
> the growth of people and which are themselves
> nourishing. There is a way of exercising authority,
> of discerning and even running the finances which
> is in the spirit of the Gospel and the Beatitudes
> and so makes these tasks sources of life.
>
> JEAN VANIER[2]

Alone with the Alone

I am going to lure her and lead her out into
the wilderness and speak to her heart. (Ho 2:14)

When the Desert Fathers in the fourth-century Egyptian desert were asked what was needed for perfection in life, the reply given was: "Go, sit in your cell, and your cell will teach you everything." Obviously this does not mean that the priest or deacon in his parish should act exactly like the desert monks of the fourth century, that would be ludicrous. However, there are certain lessons that may be learnt. There are many times when the priest may find himself alone. This may be in the presbytery after the last strains of groups of people have died away. It may be when he stands alone in the sacristy. The sacristy, of course, can often be a busy place – where people look for a word of advice from the priest, look for Mass cards, ask for Confession. But when he stands alone in the sacristy he is in a uniquely priestly position. It is then that it can be a place of silence and brotherly communion. When he stands alone before Mass he is able to be aware of priests all over the world standing ready to celebrate the sacred mysteries. Some stand in very difficult situations; some stand experiencing personal health problems; others in areas of great poverty; others again in places where the Church is persecuted. We are brothers. We are not colleagues, but brothers. In the sacristy we stand in brotherly communion in different countries, in different time zones, in different cultures, in the one Church.

The confessional too can often be a place where the priest is alone. This can happen when he sits and waits, and no one comes. It is too easy to leave the confessional when there is no one there. Or, to increase the likelihood of a confessional queue by attaching a short confession time to a slot before or after Mass. However, if we can realise that we are ministering to people even when they are not there, then we are conscious of being alone with the Alone, and bringing our parishioners into that sacred space with us. Perhaps it takes a confidence of faith to sit and wait. Being alone with God is not isolation, it is an act of giving ourselves to God and at the same time giving ourselves to God's people.

I abandoned and forgot myself,
Laying my face on my Beloved;
All things ceased;
I went out from myself,
Leaving my cares
Forgotten among the lilies.

St John of the Cross[3]

BUILDING ON EACH OTHER'S WORK

I did the planting, Apollos did the watering,
but God made things grow. (1 Co 3:6)

One of the good things for us to remember in our pastoral ministry is that we are not in competition with each other. In other words, when we arrive in a new parish we are not competing with any of our predecessors. Instead, we build on each other's work. We may be very different from the person who went before us. He would have lived at a different time, with perhaps different circumstances and with other concerns. Each of us needs to respond to the needs of the parish as they present themselves to us in our own time. In this way we are building on the work of others and respecting their memory. Of course, none of this entails that we copy those who have gone before us – that would be false. We need to be true to ourselves. However, if we are attentive to the needs of our parish community we will approach these responsibilities with enough humility towards those who have preceded us. The reason why this is important is that we are not simply dealing with the different approach of our earlier brothers, we are commenting, even if inadvertently, on the relationships built up by our brothers and their, now our, parishioners.

Having the humility to build on each other's work is to open ourselves to the inspiration of the Holy Spirit.

We may plant and water, but it is God who brings the growth. What a parish community needs before any ideas of ours, is the giving of ourselves. Therefore, regardless of whether our ideas are creative or unimaginative, people will hear the challenging words of the Gospel through us: "Come, follow me." We are co-workers in building the city of God. Except that this lofty aim may often be able to be lived only in very simple terms – recognising that we are, as Pope Benedict said on the evening of his election, humble workers in the vineyard of the Lord.

> What is it that unites a community? Isn't it its mission, which is also its goal? If there is a lack of clarity about the community's vocation and purpose, it is harder to live together.
>
> JEAN VANIER [4]

CELEBRATING SACRAMENTS

Praise God in his Temple on earth… (Ps 150:1)

One of the things that the Second Vatican Council did for the liturgy was to free it from excessive ritual, a type of ritual that had become so detailed in its prescriptions that the value of the ritual was lost in a ritualism. Along with the mechanistic thinking that it was enough to celebrate the sacraments because the very act would be sufficient to provide grace for the participants this ritualism encouraged the view that good liturgy was about exactness. The Council released us from such a constriction on our expressiveness. Clearly this does not invite us to disregard what is rubricised in the liturgical books; nor does it point the way to a neo-rubricism. Instead, it demands that we approach the celebration of the sacraments faithful to the mind of the Church. Of course, this is much more than rubrics. It challenges us to lead the parish community in prayer in such a way that we will help people to celebrate the Faith of the Church with fidelity, but also with beauty, with warmth, with humanity. This is not easy. Many factors will make this a task that is sometimes easy, sometimes very difficult. Therefore, the removal of the pre-conciliar rubricism has brought its own demands.

Perhaps a useful way of examining how we celebrate the sacraments would be to ask ourselves how well every part of the celebration contributes to the whole. For example, how possible would it be for us to present every part of the Mass as an element of thanksgiving? Is the Penitential Rite at Mass simply a part of the Introductory Rites, with a focus on fault-finding, or is it a Eucharistic element with the focus on thanking God for his mercy? Is the homily a talk given after the Gospel, or is it a prayerful occasion to thank God for revealing himself to us in his holy Word? Is the post-communion period the time for getting ready to leave, or have a second collection, or is it when the parish community sits quietly enjoying God's, and each other's, presence?

> Rubricism consists in carrying out the instructions
> to the letter, but without putting even one's self
> into it, let alone one's faith or one's piety.
>
> JEAN LEBON[5]

CELIBACY

I sleep but my heart is awake.
I hear my Beloved knocking. (Sg 5:2)

How often we hear discussions about celibacy by people who do not know what it is like. Of course, many people live celibate lives. Married people also live in many periods of sexual continence. But what makes our situation different is that we have taken a solemn promise, we have committed ourselves to a celibate way of life. However, even among ourselves we often find that the reasons we give to others for a life of celibacy are not much more than expressing the view that it gives us more time to devote the whole of life to the priestly ministry. Surely that is not enough.

Celibacy is more than a way of freeing time. It is an attitude which enables us to be loved by God and to try to love him in return, in every area of our lives. Celibacy is a way of loving. If we were to see it only as an availability mechanism, then it would be reduced to the functional. And, with that approach we might start to confuse it with a bachelor lifestyle. The celibate priest or deacon is not a bachelor. But it could be an easy mistake to make. What makes celibacy profitable for the world is when it is lived in such a way that the at-times emptiness is not filled up by bachelor-like activities. A celibate love, like all expressions of committed love, involves bearing the pain of love when it is confusing and disturbing and uncertain.

Sometimes this celibacy means facing the emptiness of a lonely life. This may be a loneliness which tempts us with other possibilities. Celibate love bears the ache of facing the walls that surround us; it looks into the darkness. On occasions we may watch television to escape, or we may visit others. But the challenge will always be to struggle with the celibate ache. This, however, is not a negative or dismal approach to life. If it were, then we might just complain about our lot. No. Being prepared to engage with the empty darkness is where we find Jesus, the Lord of Life waiting for us. "Have you seen the one whom my heart loves?" (*Sg* 3:3) Do not live in the superficiality of a bachelor priesthood. Have the courage to struggle with a celibacy that demands more and more of your life. Trust that the one whom your heart loves will be waiting for you.

> Besides contemplative prayer, the celibate life-style also asks for voluntary poverty. A wealthy celibate is like a fat sprinter…many married people do not take celibacy seriously because they contrast their daily struggle to pay the bills for food, house, and education with the carefree life of celibates and wonder who is really living out the witness to the Gospel.
>
> Henri Nouwen[6]

Confession and Spiritual Direction

*The woman put down her water jar and hurried back
to the town to tell the people, "Come and see a man
who has told me everything I ever did…"* (Jn 4:28-29)

If the priest or the deacon is to proclaim the Gospel with
authenticity then he needs to be aware of his own weakness,
his own sinfulness. Attempting to proclaim the Good News
without recognising that we are unworthy of the task,
can lead us to operate without the integrity which comes
from being challenged by the Gospel. An extreme example
would be to make demands on people without compassion;
that is to say, in order to respond to the situations in which
people find themselves, we need to have an appreciation
of the flaws inherent in the human condition – original
sin is not something confined to the theology lecture
room, it is rather, a way of understanding the frailty of the
human person. Another extreme example would be for the
priest or deacon to excuse everything a person does. This
might be justified as a way of being kind. However, if the
consequence is that the person has not been encouraged
to grow, then has the priest or deacon failed to proclaim
the Gospel?

So, how do we try to be sure that we are calling people
to grow in God's presence? The answer perhaps lies in the
awareness of our human imperfections. We, like everyone
else, are only earthenware vessels. Urging people to use the

Sacrament of Penance and Reconciliation will surely be more authentic if we ourselves are in the habit of going to Confession. Might we also find occasions to mention that we have been to Confession? Sometimes when parishes have Reconciliation Services, or Confession days, it can happen that people see one priest going to Confession to another. Obviously it would not be proper to do this just so that it would present a good example; however, when it does happen people are usually uplifted by seeing their pastors declaring themselves to be sinners, and also ministering to each other.

Furthermore, in terms of our faith development, do we think of spiritual direction as something for those with problems? Or, do we recognise that it is an important element in our journeying into the depths of God's love?

> In prayer, we need to show to the Holy Spirit what worries us and what sometimes assails our heart. The human heart is so often haunted by anxiety… in prayer we are offered the gift of surrendering everything to God, in a communion with him that brings us close to the invisible.
>
> BR ROGER OF TAIZÉ[7]

CREATIVE SPACE

Come from the four winds, breath; breathe in these dead; let them live. (Ezk 37:9)

There always seem too many things to be done. We may feel that we never manage to clear the office desk of everything that needs a response: bills, advertising promotions, monthly accounts, notices for the bulletin. We can tell ourselves that if we could clear all of these things, never mind the visits to the school and housebound, then we would have time to do other things more of our choosing. What if we decided to write into our daily timetable time for something else? This might be called 'creative time'. It would be a time for doing something else, for doing the very things we would do if we completed all of our other tasks. This could be a time for serious reading, or for writing, or simply for exploring new ideas. It would definitely not be what is sometimes these days called 'me time'. It would not be a time for laziness, but for creativity. In other words, it would be programming into our day something which would help us to keep fresh our response to God's call to share his life. This space would be very different for different people. It would not be an escape from our priestly or diaconal life – we cannot have two lives. Everything needs to have the possibility of helping us to walk in God's presence.

The idea of having a creative space encourages us to see that if our pastoral ministry is so busy at the expense of our search for God, then we need to re-balance things. It is when we allow space for the Spirit to breathe in us that we can be renewed daily in our ministry.

My Beloved is the mountains,
The solitary wooded valleys,
The strange islands,
The rushing rivers,
The breath of the loving breeze,
The night at rest
At the coming of the dawn,
The silent music,
The audible solitude…

ST JOHN OF THE CROSS [8]

Daily Mass and Prayer without the Priest

They went as a body to the Temple every day… (Ac 2:46)

In the post-Vatican II period we are used to saying that the Mass does not belong to the priest. It is the celebration of the parish community which is led by the priest. Yet we can slip into a way of thinking which still suggests that it is the 'property' of the priest. We can find different reasons why we do not need to say daily Mass. This mentality betrays an underlying mind-set which belongs to the world of ecclesial obligations.

Perhaps we need to start from somewhere else. A useful starting point would be seeing that the parish community gathered for prayer each day is what sustains our parish. It doesn't need to be at the same time of day. But it is important that the community gathers for prayer. When most of the parish community is involved at work, or school, or with domestic tasks, or are housebound, this daily prayer is a way of a few people keeping the prayer going. In this way the parish community is always at prayer – for that to happen it does not need everyone to be present in the one building, at the one time. Nor does the priest need to be there all the time. There will be legitimate reasons for the priest's absence. However, do we want a situation in which the community cannot gather for prayer just because the priest is not present? Surely not. When the priest is not able to be present for the celebration of Mass with the parish community the community can still be a visible sign of the parish at prayer. This can happen in different ways: Morning Prayer from the Divine Office; the Rosary, or other seasonal devotions; Eucharistic Adoration.

Eucharistic Adoration is particularly good because it keeps the prayer focused on the Holy Eucharist, and at the same time helps people to grow in their love for the Eucharist. It also encourages the growth of a spirituality of waiting – waiting for the return of the celebration of Mass. The practice in some quarters of taking the distribution of Communion out of Mass is a poor substitute for Mass. Indeed, the too ready acceptance of it might even blur the Mass itself. So, learning to wait together as a parish community at prayer is not only practical, it is also pedagogically sound, and fundamentally ecclesial.

> Christ is present in his Church at prayer: for it is he who is praying for us, is praying in us and is prayed to by us.
>
> — St Paul VI[9]

Deacons

I give you a new commandment: love one another.
(Jn 13:34)

One of the exciting areas of ministry which has been opened up for us is the role of deacons. They are often referred to as permanent deacons. In one sense that is unfortunate, because there are no impermanent deacons. Of course, the qualification is to distinguish them from deacons who will then be ordained priests. But ordination as a priest does not annul the ordination to diaconate. Moreover, it is a pity when seminarians, after being ordained deacons, are encouraged to think that they are 'nearly there', as if diaconate were no more than a stepping stone. Surely the time is long overdue for all of us to see that ordination by the Church to proclaim the Gospel, at diaconate ordination, is not a passing thing. Deacons who are also, but not always, married, who are employed in many different types of jobs, have brought an exciting new dimension to ordained pastoral ministry. The difficulty is that, in a functional view of ministry, the deacon is too often seen in terms of what he cannot do. It is almost as if he is viewed from a perspective that equates ordination with priesthood. In this sense the deacon is almost considered to be a limited ordained minister.

Deacons bring breadth of experience to ordained ministry. They have undergone a formation process at the same time as being fathers and husbands and workers. Theirs is an example of how the Church renews itself when it needs such a renewal. It would indeed be a shame if bishops and priests saw deacons (and if deacons saw themselves!) as limited functionaries linked to an already functional clerical body. They have the opportunity to revitalise the diocesan clergy. With their wives and families they can bring a renewed dynamic to our vision of ordained ministry. In their homes they are the clerical and lay Church working in unison.

> The diaconate emerging today is part of the larger reality of an emerging church. The challenges facing the diaconate are challenges facing the entire Church: How can we be more effective witnesses to Christ to a world so desperately in need of good news?
>
> WILLIAM T. DITEWIG [10]

Developing a Cultural Space

…and God's spirit hovered over the water. (Gn 1:2)

It is easy for our parish premises to become privatised venues – the church is used for a sacred event, or the hall is used for a social event. These involve invited people. When the premises are used in this way they have the feeling of being venues, that is to say, they open for one event, for a select group, and then are closed again. What if we could think of the premises (church and parish hall) to be a location where the whole neighbourhood might be invited to discover a varied sense of the spiritual. This would mean that the church building would be open, of course, for quiet prayer. It would also mean that the parish hall, or the church, might be used for art exhibitions, book clubs, concerts. In other words, instead of seeing that the only possibilities are for liturgy or social events, we might recognise the value of encouraging cultural events. Art is not for a limited number of aesthetes. It is for everyone. This realisation opens the way for us to proclaim the Good News to our neighbourhood in a language which may be closer to them than a sacralised one. In this way we can help people to have a sense of the sacred which would be wider than what they would expect in a religious ceremony.

Seeing our premises as a cultural space would mean that we have a greater possibility of being the hub of our neighbourhoods. People would feel comfortable being around us. Even those who would never come to liturgical or devotional ceremonies might be coaxed to discover some sense of the sacred through art or music or literature. Indeed, they might find that they already had a sense of the sacred in their everyday lives, but had not yet learnt a language to articulate it.

> [In the Middle Ages] On Sundays and during services all the inhabitants of the town might meet there, and the contrast between the lofty [church] building and the primitive and humble dwellings in which these people spent their lives must have been overwhelming. Small wonder that the whole community was interested in the building of these churches and took pride in their decoration.
>
> E.H. GOMBRICH[11]

DEVOTIONS

…when you have a party, invite the poor, the crippled, the lame, the blind… (Lk 14:13)

In recent times there has been, in some quarters, an attempt to sophisticate the forms of prayer of parish communities. It is almost as if the simple forms which might have existed in the past were in a way deficient, or not 'clever' enough, or for the uneducated. As a consequence of that mentality devotions were side-lined. Some people then began to express the view that Mass should always be said where there might previously have been devotions. It is arguable now that the Mass itself has become a devotion. Here the distinction between devotion and liturgy is crucial.

In *Evangelii Gaudium* Pope Francis speaks of the importance of popular devotions. Part of ministry of the priest may be to encourage such popular devotions. Of course, it does not mean that he needs to lead them all himself. This is a very good area in which lay people may be able to take responsibility for prayer in the parish community. For the priest or the deacon it is an opportunity to find forms of devotion which will attract people. It also allows more scope, than liturgy might, to be expressive and creative. In this way he can help people have an emotional element to their public prayer.

People like to kiss the cross on Good Friday, so why not the kissing of icons at other times of the year? They like the candle-lit church at Easter, so why not processions with candles inside the church at other times? People like the Stations of the Cross, why not encourage groups, or individuals, within the parish to write and lead the Stations of the Cross? The possibilities may not be endless, but are certainly many.

> The Aparecida Document describes the riches which the Holy Spirit pours forth in popular piety by his gratuitous initiative.... It is truly a spirituality incarnated in the culture of the lowly.
>
> — POPE FRANCIS[12]

Divine Office

From East to West, praised be the name of [the Lord].
(Ps 113:3)

"O God, come to our aid," may simply be the words we use to begin the Divine Office, yet they are much more. They are a cry during the course of the day to God who is so close that we live and move in his presence. And, in the early morning: "Lord, open our lips." We even have to ask the Lord to help us speak to him our words of praise. With these introductory pleas we enter into the Prayer of the Church. It is the way the Church has prayed for centuries. This is something worth remembering – we are not engaging in innovation, or something private. In praying the psalms we are uniting ourselves with our brothers and sisters who have gone before us. But more than that we are using some of the words Jesus, our Lord and Saviour used.

Remembering these things helps us to appreciate that whenever we pray we pray as the Church. We never pray alone. The Office helps us to have a sense of being with others, even if we appear to be alone. Like the monks and nuns who sing the psalms, side by side, in their choir stalls, we say the Office with all of our brothers and sisters who have promised, like us, to say it. Sitting, or kneeling, or standing alone we are joined in the choir stalls of the universal Church – in Asia, the Americas, Africa, everywhere. Similar to the monks and nuns in their monasteries, we chant the psalms in the church without walls. "Praise [the Lord] all nations, extol him all you peoples." (*Ps* 117:1)

However, in case it seems that this prayer is only for those who have promised to say it, it is important to note that many parish communities now recite the Divine Office. There are many lay people who recite it at home. After all, it is the Prayer of the Church, not a part of the Church but the whole Church.

> In its oldest form the office consisted of psalms and silent prayers, and was organically related to the rest of the day with its simple manual labour accompanied by 'meditation' – which meant the spoken repetition of scriptural passages – interspersed with prayer. The essence of the office was the periodic realisation in a communal form of the spontaneous, unceasing dialogue with God...
>
> DANIEL REES, ET AL.[13]

ECUMENICAL RELATIONS

Jesus said to him, "You must not stop him: anyone who is not against you is for you." (Lk 9:50)

One of the things which has always attracted me to Taizé has been their commitment to reconciliation. The brothers of Taizé have not become cynical or despondent about their appeal to all Christians to work for reconciliation. In parish situations it is easy, I think, to give up on the work of ecumenism; or if we do not give up, we can still find ourselves going through the motions. It is too easy to settle for a relationship of politeness with others. Surely that is not enough. It is also easy to tell ourselves that nothing much happens with ecumenical dialogue, and so we should not bother. I think these responses are misguided. Ecumenical dialogue must always be good. It is not a dialogue between institutions but a dialogue between brothers and sisters. This may be considered a small point; however, I think it is significant. If we hold onto the view that there is one Church – and I do not mean that in any insensitive way – then we will see each other as brothers and sisters who, at the moment, are not sharing the common meal with each other. We would not appreciate such a situation in our families, so why in our family which is the Church? One of the images which remains clear in my mind is of the papal visit of Pope Benedict in 2010, particularly the meeting he had with the Archbishop of Canterbury and others at Lambeth Palace. The obvious warmth of relations was clear for all to see. Pope Benedict and Archbishop Rowan Williams appeared comfortable with each other. We have already come a long way.

My feeling about ecumenism finds another encouragement from Taizé. When Brother Roger and his companions settled at Taizé during World War II, one of the first things he did was to offer shelter to Jews who were in peril of their lives from the Nazis. So, it seems to me that from the beginning of Taizé inter-faith dialogue has existed alongside ecumenical dialogue. Their work for reconciliation means that their commitment to the Gospel of Jesus loses nothing when they strive for reconciliation within the human family.

If at this point it sounds as if these concerns are all too big, then please be assured that I am not advocating that each of us tries to do universal things, but we can attempt to do very local things.

All men form but one community. This is so because all stem from the one stock which God created to people the entire earth, and also because all share a common destiny, namely God.

Nostra Aetate[14]

Finding Silence

Speak [Lord] your servant is listening. (1 S 3:9)

One of the challenges we can face in our everyday life is to find silence. This can be difficult not least because there may be many people who want to speak to us. It would be easy if we could programme all of our meetings with people, but that is not the way parish life works. Often people come just at the very time we have set aside to do something that requires our attention.

Finding silence is not easy. However, it is worth making a serious effort to have it in our lives. I am not saying that we should not enjoy television or radio, or listening to music. What I am saying is that these things can too easily become a way of escaping from the demands of silence. Silence is not easy. It does not allow us to avoid ourselves. It gives space for our false selves to trouble us. And, after we have gone beyond the initial delight in the silence, we can find that it challenges us to face our negativities, to go deeper into ourselves.

This attempt to create an environment of silence in the place where we live takes courage. It means that we try to live in a silence which will be conducive to the life of prayer. The physical silence involves not having constant noise. It also means that when we find the silence hard, we do not fill it with sounds, but stay with it. This is not easy. In fact, it can sometimes be painful; it is always valuable.

In this environment of valued silence our everyday tasks can become elements of our prayer. In other words, the silence is not simply a helpful atmosphere in which to pray – the silence can become the prayer. In this way we have the opportunity to pray without ceasing, as St Paul advocated.

In the silence we present ourselves to the Holy Spirit as people ready for transformation. No longer distracted by our escapist media we can be attacked by the demons. They do not bother us when we are living on the surface; however, once we attempt to move deeper, they target us. In this sense, trying to live with as much silence as possible is not an easy option. But none of this should frighten us. When we find the courage to live with silence, we discover that Jesus, who went off to a lonely place to pray, is with us. Thus the silence becomes a sharing in his presence.

Thomas Merton, monk and writer, told his novice monks that if they wanted to learn how to pray, they needed to learn how to close doors properly. His friend, the Buddhist monk and writer Thich Nhat Hanh, said that his young monks had to learn how to pour tea for the older monks with respect. In this way the pouring of the tea would become a contemplative act. These are examples, it seems to me, of ways in which our search for silence influences our relations with each other.

It is easy to glamorise silence into something which will give us a different form of good experience. We may even start to imagine that our prayer, our response to the awareness of God's presence, can have an added dimension in silence. Yes, there are times when that may be the case. For example, there is something wonderful about sitting in silent prayer, in the church, with others. But sometimes the silence in our presbytery is hard. There are times when we would like to run away from it. There are times when we may feel alone in its grip; we may feel that the walls close in on us. When it becomes too difficult we may find release by going for a walk and escaping the intensity of the silence. But it waits for us to return. To escape it every time would mean that we would be running from the possibility of entering into the depths of God's presence. It is the blacksmith's forge of the spiritual life: around us there may seem to be nothing but darkness. This darkness which may come with our silence is the invitation to a prayer which is not only beyond words, but also beyond sensory experience. If you have the courage to persevere, it may be like looking into the blacksmith's forge where sometimes a spark of recognition flies out from the darkness. This spark may be just enough to help us wait in a silence without good feelings. And, please do not tell yourself that if you wait long enough that a good experience will come. Perhaps there will be nothing but nothing itself. Do not be afraid. It is in the darkness and silence that we have the opportunity to discover the stillness of God's all-embracing love: a love which sometimes causes us to laugh and shout; a love which sometimes brings us tears of joy; a love that sometimes leaves us resting quietly, enraptured by his presence.

Some may say that this business of finding silence is suitable to monks, but not for diocesan clergy. Certainly if we were to caricature different forms of living the Christian life, then this might be the case. And yet, many people live in homes with an unchosen silence. For them it can be a burden, sometimes too heavy to bear. When the diocesan priest takes on the search for silence he is uniting himself with the many people burdened by silence. He is offering to share their pain. It is a contemplative act of mystical love. Perhaps deacons have an opportunity to teach us how the silence may bring us closer to each other. As married men, often, they know what it is to share their lives with another person, and perhaps family, and at the same time to be conscious of being in God's presence. Therefore, whether it is in the home of the married deacon, or in the presbytery of the priest, trying to find silence becomes a proclamation of the closeness of God's presence. It is the quiet, humble joy of life.

Inner silence requires first the forgetting of self, so as to quieten conflicting voices and master obsessive anxiety, constantly beginning again as a person who is never discouraged because always forgiven.

BR ROGER OF TAIZÉ [15]

Free Time

He is like a tree that is planted by water streams…
(Ps 1:3)

One of the interesting pieces of language in the lexicon of the diocesan priest is 'day off'. It is interesting because it is never really addressed what is meant by 'off', that is to say, it does not make clear what it is that we are choosing not to do. Questioning it, however, is not the same as suggesting that the priest or deacon should not have time when he is free from routine parish duties. In fact, it is important that he has such time. Asking the question allows us to examine what use he makes of this time.

It is necessary that he is clear that he is always the ordained person. He cannot decide that for a certain time in the week he is not ordained. To do that would be unfaithful to his ordained life. Therefore, it is reasonable to say that during this time he has the opportunity to develop his own personal vocational response. This may involve visiting family and friends; it may be recreational; it may offer the space for reading or writing; it may be possible for his engagement with cultural and aesthetic activities. These will depend on his age and interests. They will all afford him the possibility of giving over his life to contemplation. In this way every part of his life will be able to be a search for God's presence; every part will be a response to God's call; every part can be a transformative experience.

For personal timetabling and management it may be useful to fix a given day, or time, or times for this to take place. However, parish life is not always so accommodating – we cannot plan when people will die. So, there has to be a certain flexibility. If it is too rigid, then we relate to our parishioners as consumers, rather than as brothers and sisters in a community of Faith. But if it is not definite enough, then we may find ourselves carried along by every circumstance. Therefore, it requires a balance. What is essential is that we do not see this time as an escape, but as a time for broadening our relationship with God. Here, again, married deacons may be our example: although the deacon may have time free from parish duties, the rest of the time is still taken up with his marital and family responsibilities. Therefore, the married deacon does not have time 'on' and 'off' his response to God's call. Perhaps the priest's time 'off' is not really that – maybe it's just a different way of time 'on'.

To lose one's own will in the will of God should be the true occupation of every man's time on earth. Only a few of us – the saints – are capable of that simplicity.

We are all one, saint and sinner. Everything we do sets the whole web of creation trembling, with light or with darkness.

GEORGE MACKAY BROWN [16]

43

Homiletics

…preaching the Gospel…is a duty that has been laid on me. (1 Co 9:16)

The Church ordains priests and deacons to proclaim the Gospel. This is something much more than reading the Gospel aloud during Mass; it is more than the giving of sermons. It is, instead, the practice of living and breathing the Good News of Jesus in every area of our lives. "If I have all the eloquence of men or of angels, but speak without love, I am simply a gong booming or a cymbal clashing." (*1 Co* 13:1) This is where it is difficult. In the early years we need to learn about structures for sermons and forms of delivery. Later we may develop a style. However, these are no substitute for trying to live the Gospel we are proclaiming. Just as we respond to God's presence in our lives, so do we need to make the preparation of our sermons an always-new response to that presence. It would lack authenticity if we were to find something to say about a particular passage of the Holy Scriptures, and then repeat it verbatim every time the passage appeared. Of course, there will be forms of expression which will repeat, but that is only because they are part of ourselves. In order that we respond afresh to the demands of preaching, it will be necessary that we do not find excuses not to preach. We may also find ourselves going further in our preparation than the material we finally present in the sermon. In this way our continuing meditation (or *ruminatio* [chewing over] as the early Cistercians termed it) on the Word of God will be part of our lifelong search for God's presence.

It would be easy to give up on this practice. It would also be easy to be satisfied with delivering something trite that required no real effort. Or, we might be tempted to be very brief in order to please some people. Thus we might tell ourselves that we were being pastorally sensitive, when, in fact, we might simply be writing sermons rather than exploring the depths of the mystery of God's Holy Word.

Persevere with your meditation on the Word of God. Know that this Word is very close: it is in our mind and in our heart.

> The word addressed to us by God is a word of love, uttered loud and clear in the full light of day, and almost menacing, so as to rouse man from his dreams and make him inwardly alive to what sounds in his ears; but it is also a secret whispered in the night, gentle and alluring, impenetrable, incredible to the most robust faith, a mystery no creature will fathom. For these voices come from eternity, sounding and echoing through all that is good and true in the inner world.
>
> HANS URS VON BALTHASAR [17]

IDENTIFYING GIFTS

Our gifts differ according to the grace given us. (Rm 12:6)

It is correct to consider that we need our parishioners to help us in the work of the parish. However, there is a difficulty if we see them as doing no more than supplying those things which we do not have sufficient time to deliver. If, then, there were plenty of priests would we exclude our parishioners? Therefore, it would seem to be reasonable that we see our parishioners as doing something more than filling in the gaps of missing clergy. People have gifts that have been given to them by the Holy Spirit. The gifts were given to be used.

We all have gifts. They are not in competition with each other. They are a way in which the Spirit of the Living God reveals himself to us. So, the use of our gifts for the good of the Church does not credit our abilities; but rather it celebrates God's presence among us. And, when we rejoice in these gifts we are hearing the music of the angels, and are gliding in a cosmic dance.

These gifts, then, are so important that it is part of the ministry of priests and deacons to help people discover them. This is not a nebulous pietism – helping people to find the gifts given them by the Spirit opens them up to the giftedness which is deep down inside them. How do we do that? We do it by seeing our parishioners not as people to fill in, but as people who have something to offer which we may not have. We encourage them to be creative, if that is what they are. We give them room to manage if that is what they can do. Then we begin to recognise that we are a community of believers. We are not just a group of individuals who gather in the same building for the celebration of Mass. We are the living Body of the Risen Christ.

> To love people is to recognise their gift and to help them use and deepen it. A community is beautiful when all its members are using their gifts fully.
>
> — Jean Vanier [18]

Leader or Servant

The greatest among you must be your servant. (Mt 23:11)

Being clear about the position we hold in the parish community may not always be straightforward. There will be people who would like us to be leaders who would make things happen. This is something which it is easy to accept. It allows people to let the priest get on with doing things; it gives the priest carte blanche to act as a parochial autocrat. Moreover, it plays to the people who do not want lay people to do anything. In terms of parish structure it creates a person-dependent model. Like all person-dependent models it will ultimately fail. How attractive it is for the priest, or deacon, to tell himself that he is a leader and that people need him to lead! When this takes place there is a disconnect between the clergy and the laity. The clerics become functionaries, the laity become passive bystanders.

Perhaps a better way of thinking about himself would be for the priest, or deacon, to think of himself as a *paterfamilias*, an almost abbatial responsibility appropriate to a parish community. In this way he would think of himself, and encourage others to think about him, as an equal member of the parish community. Instead of pointing the way to a life with God, he would take the hands of his fellow travellers and walk with them into the mystery of God's love. Thus he would find himself no longer a leader, but now a servant. And, as a servant of the parish community he would learn from his fellow pilgrims as together they moved deeper into God's presence. In this learning process he would keep discovering, in new ways, what it means to be a disciple.

> A disciple is…simply a learner; and this, ultimately, is what the disciple learns: how to be a place in the world where the act of God can come alive.
>
> ROWAN WILLIAMS [19]

Lectio Divina as a Model for Ministry

Unless a wheat grain falls on the ground and dies,
it remains only a single grain; but if it dies, it yields
a rich harvest. (Jn 12:24)

Enjoyed and nurtured for centuries by our monastic brothers and sisters Lectio Divina is now being discovered by many other members of the Church. For a long time, of course, it was not open to many people simply because they could not read. Thus any form of prayer which was predicated upon the initial activity of reading (*lectio*) was closed to those who had not had the opportunity of education. Does that mean, therefore, that they were unable to experience the fruits of this Lectio Divina? No, I do not think that would be an accurate assessment. They were still able to reflect on the Scriptures as they had been told to them, and as they had experienced the mystery in their lives. The value of Lectio Divina comes not from its intellectual engagement but from the way in which it invites the person to find himself or herself in the Sacred Scriptures, then after internalising the Scripture, to take it into the rest of life. In this way our approach to life can be a living, breathing, moving Lectio Divina. Therefore, in taking the Scriptures into our lives we are like the medieval monk copying out the Gospel texts. Such monks decorated the pages on which they wrote. Sometimes they wrote other things alongside the sacred text. Thus the Gospel became a part of the monk, and in his writing the monk expressed the Gospel not simply as words, but the Word of Life became incarnate in the person of the monk.

The basic format is *lectio*, *meditatio*, *oratio*, and sometimes *contemplatio*. *Lectio*: this involves reading the words before us. *Meditatio*: this is where we respond to the text and engage with it. The early Cistercian monks also speak of *ruminatio*. Coming from their rural environment they were able to consider that as some of the animals chewed over their food, ruminated it, so too the monks could chew over the sacred text. *Oratio*: in the presence of the Word of God we offer our prayer. This may be words used as a prayer, or it may be the giving of ourselves to God in our awareness of being in God's presence. *Contemplatio*: sometimes this is spoken of as being a part of Lectio Divina; sometimes it is not. And, it is not easy to pin down. One way is just to remember that prayer is our response to being in God's presence, or "the raising of the mind and heart to God" as the Catechism says. Therefore, a useful way of considering *contemplatio* is to see that after we have engaged with the Scriptures we can carry around with us the fruits of our engagement. In this way the Sacred Scriptures become incarnate in us, and we like Mary carrying the Word of God in her womb to Elizabeth, are able to carry the Word to the people and places in our lives.

A growing number of priests and deacons have formed Lectio Divina groups in their parishes. These are usually received well by those who are involved. But maybe there is another angle. Perhaps priests and deacons might see that the Lectio Divina model has a value in the way they see their vocational response. This could be done by considering the tasks in which we are involved as a sort of *lectio*, a reading of life as it presents itself before us. How we respond to it could be thought of as a kind of *ruminatio* (*meditatio* plus *oratio*). This helps us to see that everything we do for our parishioners can be a dwelling with the Incarnate Word. Thus our parish ministry becomes more than a series of tasks, it has the possibility of being a part of our awareness of living in God's presence – this is *contemplatio*. For the diocesan priest or deacon we might even consider that the model be expressed as *lectio, cura animarum, contemplatio* – we read the signs of the Eternal Word written in our parish situations (*lectio*), we respond to it by responding to our parishioners' needs (*cura animarum*), we are nourished and satisfied as we move and live in God's presence (*contemplatio*). To give ourselves over to this contemplation is to search for God's presence in every area of our lives; it is to allow ourselves to be loved by God, even, perhaps especially, when life is confused or difficult. Our parishioners become the sacred text. The Word of God is incarnated in their lives. We read this living, moving, sacred text, finding God's presence in our relations with our parishioners. It is a living *lectio*. Our care for them (*cura animarum*) is our response to the Word of God and at the same it is wrestling with the Word as it is revealed through others. It is a living *meditatio*.

When we pray with them, and walk with them, and listen to them, and laugh with them, we are offering our prayer to God. It is a living *oratio*. So, when we are attentive to the needs of our parishioners, we are giving ourselves over to God's presence. It is a living *contemplatio*.

I and Pangur Bán, my cat,
Tis a like task we are at;
Hunting mice is his delight,
Hunting words I sit all night.
…
Practice every day has made
Pangur perfect in his trade;
I get wisdom day and night
Turning darkness into light.

ANONYMOUS, EIGHTH CENTURY [20]

MARY, THE CONTEMPLATIVE

…let what you have said be done to me. (Lk 1:38)

Whenever people argue about the ordination of women, it can often be an expression of the view that somehow the highest form of Christian living is found in the exercise of the priesthood. This is, of course, not true. Indeed, the counter-argument might be that the 'highest' form is the one which is the most humble. These debates can arise when people identify the ability to perform certain duties as what matters, when, in fact, what matters is the journey into the Mystery of God, and the inviting of others to share that journey with us. Therefore, it may be said that contemplativeness is the 'highest' form. And, this is open to everyone. Mary, gave her *fiat* to God through the Angel Gabriel; she stood in silence under the cross of Jesus; she rejoiced at the fulfilling of God's purposes in the resurrection; she was the contemplative par excellence. Mary, then, is not only our companion on the journey into the Mystery of God, she is also the one who shows us the way. She lived with such a simple and beautiful openness to God's presence that the very presence of God was able to be incarnated in her. But this openness did not depend on how she felt. It relied upon a commitment to God who was not going to abandon her. If there are occasions when we might be tempted to rely on something other than God's presence, Mary comes to us to encourage us to persevere in love for the One who is Love itself.

Mary,
be our example of living quietly
and joyfully
in God's presence.
Help us to breathe
with the very Breath of God,
allowing this Holy Spirit
to enliven us in our ministry,
and to confirm us
in our search
for God's presence.
Encourage us
to be happy
being servants
of God's people.

Fr Gerard Bogan

Mysticism and the Saints

…the temple of God is sacred; and you are that temple.
(1 Co 3:17)

Mysticism is something that may seem far removed from the lives of many priests and deacons. They may think that it belongs to the monk in his or her monastery, the anchorite in her cell, or the hermit in his poustinia. Thomas Merton said that all Christians were called to share in the contemplative life. The people, at the time, who disagreed with him argued that it was dangerous to open people up to such intensity of religious experience. Here would not be the place to examine the precise differences between the contemplative life and mysticism. It is enough to say that knowledge of things about God is no substitute for immediate experience. Indeed, this is what different forms of devotions tried to do. It was the attempt to make accessible the God who was both transcendent and immanent.

Priests and deacons have opportunities to help people open themselves to the mystical dimension. The celebration of the sacraments can easily become a matter of accurate ritual carrying the promise of grace. However, simple things can help people to have an awareness of the closeness of God's presence. The Litany of the Saints prayed when we are celebrating the Sacrament of the Sick with one of our sick brothers or sisters increases the sense of being part of the Communion of Saints. Maybe we have grown shy of the simplicity of the Litany of the Saints, with its repetition of "pray for us". And yet people like it. It is also easy. If people have been away from the practice of the Faith and are unsure of anything but the basic prayers, a simple "pray for us" involves and includes them. This is also the case when saying the Rosary in the home of someone who has died. Not only is it easy to say, it helps people to sense the closeness of the saints – they can feel something of the fullness of the Church. This may not be the *nada*, the nothingness, of St John of the Cross, but still it has a simple mystical quality about it. In any case, is mysticism not at its heart the movement, in simplicity, to the singularity of being which is perfect love?

> God…issues a summons, not to flee from the world
> but to flee with the world to the kingdom of God,
> that is, to the anticipation of the kingdom of God
> in this world; a world made whole, a world as God
> wants to see it.
>
> Edward Schillebeeckx [21]

Obedience

…rejoice rather that your names are written in heaven.
(Lk 10:20)

It would be easy to draw distinctions between the canonical obedience of the Diocesan priest and that of the professed Religious. But that might make too-easy comparisons. Perhaps it would be better for us to see that the obedience promised by the deacon and priest at ordination is a commitment to respond to the continuing demands of the Gospel, and to his vocational response, in dialogue with his bishop. It cannot mean that the bishop exerts power over the priest or deacon. Nor does it allow the priest or deacon to treat his bishop as a schoolboy might his head teacher. It needs to be an honest dialogue. In this dialogue the bishop, in a fatherly way, helps the priest or deacon in his personal search for God, and in his pastoral ministry. In return the priest or deacon tries to see the invitation of the Holy Spirit working through his bishop. Thus the dialogue becomes a faith-filled encounter in which two people see themselves journeying together.

This may not always be easy. Indeed, if it is an honest dialogue, it will be beset by the types of distractions which attempt to derail any such relationship. However, the difficulties should never be glossed over, in a desire for a comfortable *modus vivendi*. Such an attitude would be the polite exchange of work colleagues, but it would not be the engagement of disciples. A true engagement will often be challenging for both parties. It will not allow the individual to settle for an easy way, but will call him to steer away from the false self that individualism might seek to construct.

A useful perspective can be found in monastic communities: the community elects the abbot/abbess, then agrees to be under his/her obedience. In this way the abbot or abbess is aware of being an equal member of the community, and the monks are supportive of the responsibility they have asked their abbot to carry. This is not the same, of course, as a diocesan situation; however, it may offer us an insight from another part of the Church of the way in which bishops, priests and deacons might relate to each other.

> By obedience we do not renounce our freedom;
> we dedicate it to God; we promise to use it in the
> service of God alone and for his honour and glory,
> with the explicit understanding that *servire Deo
> regnare est* [to serve God is to reign] that to obey
> God with freedom is man's highest dignity; it
> enables him to grow and mature spiritually.
> THOMAS MERTON[22]

Open Church

Oh, come to the water all you who are thirsty. (Is 55:1)

A renewed appreciation of the life of prayer – prayer as the community of believers, prayer on our own – is what will transform our parish communities. On 16th October 1978, just after St John Paul II had been elected Pope, he stood on the balcony and said: "Open wide the doors to Christ." Later, Pope Benedict reminded us of these words. Now Pope Francis is asking us to open the doors of our churches. By this he does not simply mean for us to have an open disposition. He does that when he says: "The Church [capital C] is called to be the house of the Father, with the doors always wide open." But then he gives clear practical guidance when he says: "One concrete sign of such openness is that our church [small c] doors should always be open, so that if someone, moved by the Spirit, comes there looking for God, he or she will not find a closed door."[23] Of course, it is easy for us to complain that the life of the Church is not as it was once. We can slowly become used to complaining, and in the process be beaten down by a sense of hopelessness. A first step is to open our church buildings. After that we give people not only the chance to pray in the quiet church, but we also offer people the opportunity to be taught how to pray in silence. The open church building is a sign to all around us that we are inviting people to share God's life; it is a sign of God's presence; it opens not just the building but our hearts to the wonders of God's presence.

Why are we waiting? Just imagine all the Catholics in our country, and our friends in the wider Christian Family, were to commit themselves to prayer. Just imagine all the church buildings were to become places of prayer and solitude for the whole society. Just imagine our church buildings were seen as a place to learn to meet Jesus, the Risen Christ. Just imagine we stopped imagining and started to do. This would be the joy of the Gospel.

[Archbishop Thomas Becket:]
Unbar the doors! throw open the doors!
I will not have the house of prayer,
   the church of Christ,
The sanctuary, turned into a fortress.
The church, shall be open, even to our enemies.
Open the door!

T. S. ELIOT [24]

Pastoral Planning

Make a straight highway for our God across the desert.
(Is 40:3)

One of the difficulties with the idea of pastoral planning is that we may be resistant if we feel that it is being imposed upon us from somewhere else. That is understandable. We may object by saying that our situation is different from all of the others. This may be partially correct – we would not want to deny the uniqueness of our particular parish communities. At the same time we need to recognise that there are also many shared characteristics. So, pastoral planning may have common threads, but it needs to be local, and it needs to exist. If we were not to have any planning then we would be at the mercy of every situation that arose. Then we might tell ourselves that we were really busy; and, because we were so occupied there would be no room for creativity or innovation. Whilst perseverance has many important qualities, if it is at the expense of joyfulness it can become drudgery. The Spirit is alive in us; the Spirit breathes in us; the Spirit wants us to renew the face of the Earth.

Planning in our work is good: we plan our work, then we work our plan. Any management course would guide us in that direction. However, we need to try to be clear about pastoral planning as an action of the local Church. It may have diocesan components, but true to the Church's own thinking about subsidiarity, it works best when it is pastoral action done at the most local level. What is the purpose of such pastoral planning? Who does it? Perhaps it would be useful to say that the pastoral planning team ought not to be the same people as those who do what is planned. If they were, then all that would happen would be that the planners would over-burden themselves with tasks. So, the planning team could be a team that tries to stimulate activity within the parish and at the same time involve people in the delivery of what is planned. It would seek to develop a parish community in which the priest did not need to decide everything. It would be a parish with a dynamic buzz. In this way it would be proclaiming the Good News. Moreover, it goes without saying that the pastoral planning is not that of the priest or deacon. He, of course, will have an essential role in the group, but it should try to be the group identifying the needs of the parish and responding to those needs. The pastoral planning in parishes may be very different from one another. It does not really matter. What does matter is that it happens.

> Like Christ [the priest] must make Christ visible in the midst of the flock entrusted to his care, having a positive and encouraging rapport with the lay faithful. … In the awareness of the profound communion which binds him to the lay faithful…the priest will make every effort to awaken and deepen co-responsibility in the one common mission of salvation, with a prompt and heartfelt esteem for all the charisma and tasks which the Spirit gives believers for the building up of the Church.
>
> CONGREGATION FOR THE CLERGY[25]

Personal Prayer

Feed me with raisin cakes, restore me with apples,
for I am sick with love. (Sg 2:5)

In our search for the presence of God in our lives it is important that we find time simply to sit in the quiet of the presence which is already with us. This will not be able to be satisfied solely by the various duties and prayers which we are obliged to do. We still need to find time which is given freely to the one who loves us. We need to find time which can be given over to him. It is a time in which we can forget about achievements, where we no longer need to meet targets and goals, where the expectations of others can be left in the far distance. In our personal prayer we can just wait in silence. It will be a silence that is sometimes uneasy because it may not provide good feelings; however, it will be drawing us beyond any reliance on sensory satisfactions. It will be the giving of ourselves to the one we love; more than that, it will be waiting for the one who loves us. This is where our priesthood is expressed not in terms of function, but in terms of being. Waiting in the presence of the Holy One we are opening ourselves to the Spirit of the Risen Christ. We are expressing our desire to be changed, to be loved, to be held, to be understood, to be accepted, to be forgiven, to be carried into the mystery of the Kingdom of God.

This is the prayer of God's little ones. In this prayer we leave behind our vanities. We approach the Lord barefooted. Most of the time not much will appear to happen. It always will be happening; it may just be that we do not experience it. It is during this prayer that we are sitting in the dark – waiting for the one who loves us, just because he loves us, just because we can do no other. Caught in his love, we wait. Often we will be distracted. Often we will be tempted to go and do something. This may be because we feel that nothing is going on. However, if we find the courage to wait we will be drawn into the great Nothing – not an existential nihilism, but the place devoid of all sensory perception, maybe even the simplicity of God's presence. In this meta-sensory state we grow, very slowly, to know the Nothing as the envelopment of Love itself. In the dark we wait for the Lord to show his face. And, his face is beautiful.

> …only in prayer is the whole man there in God's immediate presence. The faith of today's priest is the man of prayer and mystical contemplation or it is nothing.
>
> KARL RAHNER[26]

Preferential Option for the Poor

I tell you truly, this poor widow has put in more
than any of them… (Lk 21:3)

When we make decisions in our parishes, are they
decisions that consciously put the poor first? When we are
promoting an excursion, or a holiday, or pilgrimage, do we
consider what impact it might have on those parishioners
who would not be able to afford to go? It is easy to talk
about the poor who live somewhere else. We may also work
according to a caricature of what we imagine 'the poor' to
be. In our parishes it may be that people are not considered
to be poor – they may be in employment and able to
see to the basic necessities of domestic living. However,
there may not be much room for luxuries. It may not be
appropriate to speak about these parishioners as the poor.
But the idea of a preferential option remains sound, that
is to say, that when we are promoting ideas they should
not be, as much as it is possible, exclusive to the affluent.
Therefore, the idea of the preferential option for the poor
is not some Marxist dialectic dressed up as evangelical
living. It is, instead, a way of being attentive not just to the
needs of our neighbour, but also to our neighbour's hopes,
aspirations, dreams, self-esteem, self-respect, position in
the parish community.

The argument may be put that 'most people can afford
it', similar to the one which says that 'most people have

cars'. A commitment to a preferential option form of ministry means that we decide for the few who cannot, rather than the many who can. Thus thinking in the way of a preferential option helps to re-orientate our parish communities according to people's needs rather than desires. In this way the whole community learns to live with an asceticism of joy and a contemplation of being in the presence of God incarnate.

> Every day I had been with people who did heavy work. I came to know their living situations, their families, their interests, their human worth, and their dignity.... I made friends with the workers. Sometimes they invited me to their homes. Later, as a priest and bishop, I baptised their children and grandchildren, blessed their marriages, and officiated at many of their funerals. I was also able to observe their deep but quiet religiosity and their great wisdom about life.
>
> St John Paul II [27]

PRIEST OR MINISTER

…but when you grow old…somebody else will put a belt round you and take you where you would rather not go.
(Jn 21:18)

Some would argue that this distinction is one which highlights a pre-conciliar and post-conciliar divide. That would perhaps be simplistic. It would also be inaccurate. Maybe it represents different attitudes. On the one hand we could speak of the priest as a cultic figure; on the other hand, we could speak of the minister as someone engaged in pastoral activity. However, if we were to consider that only one of these was correct, then we might limit our understanding of priesthood. Yes, we are ordained to celebrate the sacraments; yes, we are ordained to minister to our parishioners. It might be argued by some that in pre-conciliar days the priest understood himself to be someone who celebrated the sacraments. This would not represent the reality of the situation. Priests before the Council were also very active in encouraging pastoral initiatives – societies and clubs.

In these post-conciliar days some have argued that the priest has become too much of a minister. They would propose that the priest returns to the pre-conciliar image. Of course, once we see that before the Council the priest was both a celebrant and a facilitator of pastoral activities, any suggestion that the priest might return to the pre-conciliar cultic figure, is an erroneous one. It is an easy temptation to see the priest as someone who exercises a ministry of liturgies and devotions only; however, this sacristy mentality belongs neither to the Council's image of the priest, nor to the pre-conciliar reality. It would be something to be avoided. The architect Jack Coia once said that he didn't want young architects to learn from books and lectures alone. He said that he wanted them to take off their jackets.[28] Perhaps the same applies to priests and deacons – we need to have the dust of the street on our shoes.

Seeing ourselves, then, as people on the street ["*callejeros*" according to Pope Francis] we will see that priesthood is not the life of a celebrant but the life of one who, in ministering to people, is giving up his life. When we unite ourselves to Jesus, who is the one who sacrifices and is also the sacrifice, we present ourselves as a humble offering that only the Spirit can make fragrant. Suffused with the Breath of God we share in the priesthood which can only be understood in terms of the life, death and resurrection of Jesus.

> We can only exist as men by willingly becoming the image of Love, as manifested in Christ, who, though innocent, chose to suffer the fate of the unjust…. There is no true love of God without an unreserved acceptance of death.
>
> Brother Luc, one of the Atlas Martyrs, quoted by Dom Donald McGlynn, ocso[29]

Prophecy not Survival

Come back to me with all your heart...let your hearts be broken, not your garments torn. (Jl 2:12-13)

We have been ordained to proclaim the Gospel, to proclaim Good News, to invite people to share in the wonder of God's presence. Sometimes this means finding ways to communicate the Word of God beyond the confines of our church building or parish community. Sometimes, like the Old Testament prophets, it means calling people back into the presence which they have forgotten. When Pope John Paul, of happy memory, and Pope Benedict proclaimed the need for a new evangelisation they were encouraging us not to find new systems, but a renewed zeal, a living joy. This is not to say that we can ignore systems – they are necessary if we are to be effective. However, the system itself cannot be enough. If we imagined that it might be, then we would find ourselves tied up in dull exactitudes. Again, there is a place for exactness, for example, we cannot have quasi-orthodoxy; so, teaching must be clear. But not for its own sake. It must be clear in order to assist in the process of showing people the ideal way of living the Christian life, of living a human life, of moving towards happiness. These two estimable brothers, John Paul and Benedict, desired something much more. Each in his own way tried to express how we might share with a waiting world the joy of living and moving in the beauty of God's presence. St Paul VI too, in his apostolic exhortation *Evangelii Nuntiandi*, knew that if we were to announce it to others, we first had to live it ourselves.[30] Pope Francis, bringing a Latin American perspective to his universal ministry, challenges us to announce the simplicity and joy of the Gospel, and to avoid self-satisfaction and self-pre-occupation.

We can find ourselves caught up in trying to keep the current system going. Perhaps we need, instead, to make a radical appraisal of our very raison d'être. In other words, to have the courage to examine what we must carry with us as we set out with the seventy-two disciples to proclaim the Good News, and what is a burden that can be left behind. Furthermore, it is important to remember that it is not simply the ordained minister who has the task of offering a prophetic witness. It belongs to the whole parish community. Leonardo Boff said that in the community everyone, not just a few, should give a prophetic witness.[31] In his correspondence with the esteemed monastic historian Jean Leclercq, Thomas Merton said that the future of monasticism was not survival but prophecy. Might this not be good directional advice for diocesan bishops, priests and deacons? Concerned with survival we act as a structure, a system; concerned with prophecy we breathe deeply the Spirit who surrounds us, and vibrant with the joy of the Gospel, we announce it to others.

The Old Testament prophets were not people who were very much concerned with predicting the future.

Their concern was to call people back to a true and faithful relationship with God. This meant that they needed to enter into a process of on-going conversion – if they were to return to God, they would need to leave behind whatever distracted them from God's presence. This meant that the prophetic element was a continuing invitation and response: God invites the prophet to speak in his name and the prophet responds; the prophet then invites people to hear God's invitation and the people respond. In this way the prophetic dynamic is one in which the various people involved are in a relationship with each other which is moving and life-giving. But this prophetic dynamic may not always be easy or straightforward. It may demand that we do not cling to old ways just because they are old ways, or because we are comfortable with them, or because they have worked in the past. The prophetic element requires that our focus is God alone – God revealed perfectly in Jesus and God revealed in partial ways in other people. To cling to what has been is to hold onto what is no more, it has been. Responding to God is responding to what we do not yet know. And, that is challenging – we do not know where it will take us, or how it will work out. It costs the giving of ourselves.

Survival, on the other hand, is little more than an instinct. It is an important instinct, for we need to want to live. However, if we are not able to rise above instinct then we are not much more than the animals who also have instinct written into their being. Prophecy is where the human person shows that he or she has the potential to choose a form of living which is more than a programmed feature. The human person can relate to others in such a way that they all discover the capacity to move into deeper depths of life. Survival, on its own, has the capacity to keep us with the familiar and finally to stagnate. Of course, survival has an important part to play in our ecclesial life; however, without the prophetic element it may leave us in a cycle in which we repeat over and over again the same things without ever moving forward. Prophecy enables us to call others into God's presence and, at the same time, move closer ourselves towards divine union.

> To dedicate oneself to intraecclesial problems…
> is to miss the point regarding a true renewal of
> the Church. For this renewal cannot be achieved in
> any deep sense except on the basis of an effective
> awareness of the world and a real commitment
> to it…. To seek after changes themselves is to pose
> the question in terms of survival. But this is not the
> question. The point is not to survive, but to serve.
> The rest will be given.
>
> GUSTAVO GUTIÉRREZ[32]

Schools of Prayer

Come to me, all you who labour and are overburdened,
and I will give you rest. (Mt 11:28)

St John Paul II, of happy memory, encouraged us to make
our parishes schools of prayer. How exciting it might be if
people identified the local church as the place where people
went if they wanted to learn how to pray. They would have
the opportunity to stretch beyond the saying of particular
prayers, to knowing what it was like to sit in the silence
of God's presence. They would be able to learn what St
Teresa of Avila called the Prayer of Quiet.[33] This easy-to-
learn Quiet Prayer could be taught to young children as
well as to adults. The parish church would come to be the
place where people could learn how to draw living water
from the well where the Saviour sits offering it. Similar to
the encounter between Jesus and the Samaritan Woman
people would grow in their knowledge of Jesus. Learning
to sit quietly with the Risen Christ would open up for them
a deepened and simplified appreciation of being with God.

The parish church would be something more than the
place where the community gathered on Sundays. It would
be the oasis in the desert of the lives of many people. By
being schools of prayer we would not simply be talking
about prayer, we would be doing it; instead of pointing the
way to happiness, we would be taking people by the hand
and taking them with us. We would make the building

available for people to come and find the quiet. We would also run specific courses which would teach people Quiet Prayer. How many of our parishioners would find this a transformative experience? How many young adults would discover that there was more to the life of the Church than what is often experienced as dull ritualism? Just imagine if people came to see prayer not as a set of words, but as the path to the place where Perfect Love dwells.

...our Christian communities must become genuine 'schools' of prayer, where the meeting with Christ is expressed not just in imploring help but also in thanksgiving, praise, adoration, contemplation, listening and ardent devotion, until the heart truly 'falls in love'. Intense prayer, yes, but it does not distract us from our commitment to history: by opening our heart to the love of God it also opens it to the love of our brothers and sisters, and makes us capable of shaping history according to God's plan.... It is essential therefore that education in prayer should become a key-point of all pastoral planning.

St John Paul ii [34]

SEARCHING FOR GOD

Seek [the Lord] while he is still to be found,
call to him while he is still near. (Is 55:6)

It is easy for us to give so much time to proclaiming the Gospel and teaching it that we can forget how important it is for us to persevere in our own search for God. This search for God is our desire to know him with every part of our being: to know him in faith; to know him intellectually; to know him in our relations with each other; to know him intimately, person to person, lover to beloved. And, the search is at the same time our response to his call. We are looking for the one who wants to be found. It means not to assume that we already know him, as if he could be comprehended by us.

Studying for the diaconate and for the priesthood we may find ourselves considering what vocation means. We may think about it in terms of God calling us to ordained ministry – calling us to be a priest or calling us to be a deacon. What if we considered that God did not call us to be a something? Would that challenge us too much? Would it undermine us? I hope not. To my mind, if we think that we have been called to be a something, then we run the risk of thinking that we have arrived and that all we need to do is to keep doing the same thing. If, however, we are able to see that the call of all the baptised is to share in God's life – a call to holiness – then we have the chance to recognise that our ministry is a response to the call.[35] Why that is helpful is because it encourages us to see that the call of God and our response is something that continues. When Shakespeare *inter alios* used "*cucullus non facit monachum*"[36] [the cowl does not make the monk] he was making the point that just because someone dressed like a monk, it did not mean that he in fact was one. However, the monastic origins of the saying may be more instructive. When a monk received the cowl it was a sign that he had been received fully and permanently into the monastic community, and yet it was still important for the individual monk to know that the receiving of the cowl was not an endpoint. It was merely a recognition on the part of the community that the person was serious in his search. In a similar way, it seems to me that the moment of ordination is the point at which the community (the Church) recognises that we can be appointed to proclaim the Gospel and celebrate the sacraments. But it ought not to be thought of as an endpoint. If people who love each other try to make sure that they never change, then they usually discover that their relationship with each other becomes dry; it may even stagnate. One of the expressions which married people sometimes use is: you need to work at your marriage. Thus deacons who are married are challenged to work at their friendship with God as they work at their marriage; priests ought to work at their friendship with God, not pretending that it can remain the same, but that it needs to keep moving.

The search for God is the dynamic which vitalises the whole of our ministry. This, of course, is not a theoretical construct. Our search for God will mean that when we are preparing a sermon we will try to take our personal understanding beyond what we will deliver in the sermon; when we read, we will choose material that will develop our response to God; we will attempt to order our lives in such a way that the situation will be conducive to being aware of living in God's presence.

After a number of years in ministry there will come the point at which we know how to 'do the job'. It would be a pity if at that point we rested on our laurels. The challenge is always to grow deeper. When the Samaritan Woman met Jesus at the well, he was not only asking her for water, he was perhaps inviting her to jump into the well! He was asking her to have the courage to go into the deepest part of herself. When she jumped into the well, she would leave behind her everyday securities. She would give up the warmth of the sun. In the darkness she would not know where she was going. But when she splashed into the water, she would see her reflection and the reflection of Jesus. Washed by the presence of God, she would laugh with the joy of the one who had always loved her. Her joyful laughter, carried on the Breath of God, would be her proclamation of the Good News to the villagers which would, then, have come out of her search for God.

...the essential foundation of priestly ministry is a deep personal bond to Jesus Christ. Everything hinges on this bond, and the heart of all preparation for the priesthood and of all continuing priestly formation must be an introduction to it. The priest must be a man who knows Jesus intimately, who has encountered him and has learned to love him.

JOSEPH RATZINGER, POPE BENEDICT XVI[37]

Simplicity and Marginality

At sunset all those who had friends suffering from
diseases of one kind or another brought them to him…
(Lk 4:40)

For many people in our increasingly secularised society
the life of the priest is baffling. Some cannot understand
why we live the way we do. Others may feel sorry for us.
Others again may even find our lives to be disturbing. Part
of this view which they have of us is formed by seeing us
as unmarried men, doing religious things which belong to
a world of the past. Do they see us as a type of religious
bachelor, conducting religious ceremonies, being free from
the family responsibilities of most people, and basically
living a lonely bachelor lifestyle? Do we see ourselves that
way? Or, might we have the courage to respond to the
society around us by challenging it with our simplicity and
marginality? If we were to do that we would need to try to
live as simply as possible. We would still be considered by
many to be different, maybe even strange. But we would,
as people living on the margins of society, be a voice crying
in the wilderness.

Such a marginal way of living is not easy. Aristotle said
that those who live outside the city, on the margins, are
either beasts or gods![38] Simple living demands commitment, the type of commitment that would follow Jesus into
the outskirts of the towns where nobody lived. At least,

'nobody' according to those with power and influence and prestige and wealth. When Jesus went out into the margins of the towns, people from everywhere flocked to him. Maybe we have passed the time of trying to fit in with the wider society, telling ourselves that in such a way we might bring influence to bear. Maybe now is the time to challenge the wider society with our simplicity, with our marginal living. Then this form of asceticism for a modern world might proclaim the Gospel in a fresh way to a world lost in pleasure seeking. It is a world desperate for happiness and contentment. If we, as priests and married deacons in similar but not the same ways, were able to rise to this challenge, then the wider society might hear us not as hectoring moralising voices, but as voices of quiet joy.

> Your availability calls for a continual simplification of your way of life, not by constraint but by faith. Flee the complications through which the tempter seeks you. Throw aside all the pointless burdens, the better to bring to Christ your Lord those of your sisters and brothers.
>
> BR ROGER OF TAIZÉ [39]

STABILITAS

Stay in the same house, taking what food and drink they have to offer... (Lk 10:7)

The idea of the priest or deacon being in the one place for a lengthy period of time may be considered as anathema to some. The argument is often put that after a few years you dry up and have nothing more to give. Some might facetiously say that such an approach would suggest that we exhaust our ideas after a little while, and therefore, need to move somewhere else in order to exhaust the same ideas. That would treat pastoral ministry as if it were a list of functions to be carried out. It might also keep the priest or deacon on a level of politeness with his parishioners, never getting too close. That would be a pity; it would ignore the necessary nature of the community travelling together.

Here an example from some of our monastic brothers and sisters may help. They promise *stabilitas* [stability] in order that they may, with their community, have the steadiness of location which facilitates their engaging in the process of *conversio/conversatio morum* [changing of our ways, *metanoia*]. In other words, by rubbing up against each other, knowing that they are not just going to get up and go, they will both challenge each other to grow, and support each other in their growth. The monastic setting is, of course, a different one from a parochial setting; however, there are sufficient similarities to make it possible for one to shed light on the other. Both are ecclesial societies of people who are in a continuing struggle of *metanoia*, attempting to see more clearly the face of the Risen Christ. Thus the changing of our ways happens when we relate ever more closely to each other. The priest or deacon who sees himself performing sacred duties, without interacting on a personal level with his parishioners, will not be challenged to change his ways.

Opening ourselves to being challenged in the *conversio morum* comes about when we have enough *stabilitas* in order to facilitate growth in personal relations. Then we may discover that our ideas are not so easily exhausted, because the honest human interactions of being part of an ecclesial community will generate more ideas. This all demands attentiveness – not just to our duties, but to the Holy Spirit breathing through our parishioners. There will always be reasons why priests and deacons need to be given new appointments; however, length of stay, in itself, may not be a very good one.

> Stability involves both bearing from day to day
> the inevitable trials and disappointments which
> are part of human life and profiting from them....
> Stability ensures that he will not evade the cross,
> particularly the cross of obedience.
>
> DANIEL REES, ET AL. [40]

STUDY AND READING

And so I prayed, and understanding was given me…
(Ws 7:7)

With the many demands which are upon us in our pastoral ministry it may not always be easy to find enough time for study and reading. However, it is surely important that we try to find some time. Managing to find time for study and reading in the middle of the work we have to do means that we are always pushing ourselves beyond the immediate. Of course, the study does not need to involve an academic course. It is possible to engage in study on our own. 'Study' would mean serious reading. This might be building on something we already know, or it might be a new area. It would be easy for us to leave behind study when we leave seminary. That would be a pity. It would almost seem as if learning was a burden placed upon us, rather than the opportunity to use knowledge to construct our thinking. Indeed, the practice of study after a few years of ministry enables us to bring our pastoral experience to the study. In this way the serious reading becomes part of our ongoing meditation. It helps bring together our reflection on the world around us, the Word of God, the teaching of the Church, the celebration of the sacraments, our relations with others. Thus the commitment to serious reading is an element in our intellectual, or cognitive, response to God's showing of himself in the world around us.

It is easy to tell ourselves that there is no time for serious reading. Would that be an honest appraisal of our daily lives? What time do we give to other things? Sometimes we may just have to timetable the time. What might be this 'serious reading'? Not hefty theological tomes. It could be keeping up our spiritual reading or reading serious literature. In fact, the scope would be as broad as the range of people in ministry.

One of the good things about keeping learning, in a fairly structured way, is that it need not be public. It can simply be part of our response to the search for God's presence in our lives.

The Country Clergy

I see them working in old rectories
By the sun's light, by candlelight,
Venerable men, their black cloth
A little dusty, a little green
With holy mildew. And yet their skulls,
Ripening over so many prayers,
Toppled into the same grave
With oafs and yokels. They left no books,
Memorial to their lonely thought
In grey parishes; rather they wrote
On men's hearts and in the minds
Of young children sublime words
Too soon forgotten. God in his time
Or out of time will correct this.

R. S. Thomas[41]

Sunday Mass

These remained faithful to the teaching of the apostles, to the brotherhood, to the breaking of bread and to the prayers. (Ac 2:42)

The Sunday Mass is the time when we gather with our parish community to celebrate the Lord's Day. It is our weekly celebration of the death and resurrection of the Lord Jesus. It is more than a gathering of the local community, for we are united with the whole Church when we celebrate it. However, it is also a gathering of the local community. This is when most of the community sees each other. It is the highpoint of the parish community's week. How joyful it is that Children's Liturgies have now become commonplace at Sunday Masses. Ministers of Holy Communion too have become a part of Sunday Mass. How encouraging it is to see Holy Communion being taken to our housebound parishioners.

With more priests being given the charge of two or more church buildings, and being challenged to try to bring these different communities together, perhaps it would also be useful for us to examine the number of Masses. Rather than treating the celebration of Mass as the product of a service industry in which people are given lots of choices, maybe we could look to some of our Protestant brothers and sisters who consider it to be important that the whole community should be able to come together in one place at one time. Although we are in a different position from them, according to custom and practice, it may be an encouragement for us to recognise the value of starting from there being one Sunday Mass and then adding to it as needs require. Even the examination of this situation might help us and our parishioners to develop a fuller understanding of the Sunday Mass as an occasion where we are all together. There are still hangovers from a past that seemed to so emphasise the fulfilling of the obligation of the individual that the importance of being with the other members of the parish community was lost.

In 1996 seven Catholic monks, of the Cistercian Order, whose monastery was in the Atlas Mountains, in Algeria, were taken hostage by terrorists, and then killed. During the time when everyone was waiting for news of the monks, one of the friends of the monastery said that it was a time "to live the Eucharist more intensely".[42] Perhaps now is a time for all of us to live the Eucharist more intensely.

> The Mass is not a religious service, nor is it a family meal, nor a community feast. It is an event in which heaven and earth come together, as mundane time and sacred time are united.
>
> JOHN J. HALDANE[43]

Visiting the Sick and Housebound

Lord when did we see you…sick…and go to see you?
(Mt 25:38-9)

There are many blessings which come from visiting those who are sick and those who are housebound. Some of them may be in hospital or care homes; some may be unable to leave their own homes. But one thing that is consistent is the welcome they give us. Although unwell, they appreciate the priest, or these days also the deacon, coming to visit them. We are for them the local expression of the Church. Sometimes we will be celebrating the sacraments with them; often the visit will simply be an opportunity to have conversation. They consider it to be a blessing that the ordained minister has come to see them. For us too there is a blessing – it is the dynamic, the movement of the Spirit, in which we encounter the poor Jesus, the humble Jesus.

It would be easy to tell ourselves that we did not have enough time. What is our time for? It would also be possible to excuse ourselves with the fact that there are fewer priests than previously. Except that there is no obligation to visit as regularly as in the past. If we are in a parish with a large number of housebound parishioners, then it may be the case that we visit less frequently, but we should still visit.

It was not only Paul or Apollos or Cephas who built the Church for us. It was built by all our brothers and sisters who went before us. Some of these celebrated the Eucharist faithfully throughout their lives; then there came a point when they were unable to join the rest of the community. Is that not the point at which the rest of the community goes to them? For the administration of Holy Communion, the Ministers of Holy Communion are important. However, the priest or the deacon, as the Church's ordained ministers, are like an official presence.

What finally counts is not whether we know Jesus and his words but whether we live our lives in the Spirit of Jesus. The Spirit of Jesus is the Spirit of Love…. Jesus comes to us in the poor, the sick, the dying, the prisoners, the lonely, the disabled, the rejected. There we meet him, and there the door to God's house is opened for us.

HENRI NOUWEN[44]

WE ARE THE SAME, BUT DIFFERENT

Give, and there will be gifts for you: a full measure,
pressed down, shaken together, and running over,
will be poured into your lap… (Lk 6:38)

It may be obvious to say "we are the same, but different",
but it is still worth saying. There are many similarities in
our lives; we do many of the same things; we share the
same beliefs; and yet we are still unique human beings. It
would be a pity if, in order to express our brotherhood, we
felt the need to try to be the same. Or, if we imagined that
we ought to be the same. Even if there has to be uniformity
of practice in some areas of our ministry, there does not
need to be in every area. Nor, do we want to deny our
own personal charisms, or interests. We are brothers. That
means that we share our lives with each other, and have
responsibilities to one another, but we are still different
people. Recognising and rejoicing in our different gifts is
surely a good thing.

False humility is an easy trap to fall into. Falling into it
leads us to rubbish anyone who tries to hold onto ideals,
who expresses the joyful simplicity of the Gospel. It is an
unhealthy cynicism, perhaps born of insecurity, which
masquerades as normal, ordinary, expected ways of living.
But it is not good. Living in a consumerist society in which
human relations can be sullied by mercantilism, is it not
the ordained minister who can be a living proclamation of

the beauty of life which is more resplendent than Solomon in all his regalia? Therefore, we should try to learn from each other's gifts.

> The spiritual life of the priest and his pastoral ministry go hand in hand with [the] ongoing personal formation to deepen and harmonise the human, spiritual, intellectual, and pastoral aspects of his formation…. The activity of formation is based on a dynamic demand intrinsic to the ministerial charisma…this can never be considered finished, neither on the part of the Church which imparts it, nor on the part of the minister who receives it.
>
> CONGREGATION FOR THE CLERGY[45]

Young People

I want you to be happy, always happy in the Lord;
I repeat, what I want is your happiness. (Ph 4:4)

It is interesting that when people refer to the Latin American bishops at Puebla and Medellín making a preferential option for the poor, they tend not to refer to the preferential option for young people proposed at the same time. Of course, in our situation part of the difficulty is that it may not be clear what we might mean by young people: would it mean primary school children, or secondary school, or young adults, or young families? Maybe we should not worry ourselves with the question. If we are open to the option for young people, then we will find the age group in front of us. In one situation it may be very young children, in another young families.

Sometimes priests and deacons have asked whether we should be spending every morning in our parish churches instead of being in secondary schools. This would certainly be a big challenge for priests and deacons, but also for the parish community. It may not be the way for everyone to go; however, it may encourage us to look for ways in which we might see our young people not as the Church of the future, but as part of the Church of today.

It is easy for us to see young people as a homogeneous group for which we put on specialised events away from the parish community. What would be the reaction if we acted in the same way towards people in their fifties or sixties? Obviously there are advantages in giving some attention to young people which involves going somewhere else, but not at the expense of their feeling themselves to be a living breathing part of the parish community. Moreover, the parish community needs to experience the vitality of young people.

> Our young people want holiness; they want that complete surrender to God. They will hesitate if they expect that total surrender to God and then don't find it in us.
>
> MOTHER TERESA OF CALCUTTA[46]

Conclusion

Recently it was said to me that I seemed to be as enthused about priestly ministry as I had ever been. I agreed but then added that I did not have the same energy as I had many years ago. That means that I do things at a different pace; it also means that some things have become so much a part of who I am that there is less effort needed. Experience and energy will probably be found in different measure within the body of bishops, priests and deacons – it is not a competition. However, what I consider to be good is that at whatever stage I have been at, it has been useful to be aware of the way in which those who have gone before us have lived as ordained ministers. For that reason I have found it helpful to reflect on standard pastoral practices in the light of traditional spiritual thinking. I am not suggesting that we should always use the same language to speak of what happened in the past – that might too easily lead us into the false world of nostalgia. We need to be people of our time, not of another time.

Therefore, I am advocating that we keep looking afresh at traditional practices. I am not, however, sympathetic to ways of speaking about the spiritual and pastoral life in terms of a trendy pseudo-psychology. We are not self-help gurus. Nor should we see ourselves as religious equivalents of health professionals or care workers. Both of these groups have very important responsibilities in our society, but who we are is of another order. I like to remember the story of the monk, who when asked what use monks were, replied "no use at all". He was not saying that they were without purpose. The point he was making was that he reserved the right not to be defined according to someone's utilitarian classifications. So too with bishops, priests and deacons: we are first of all disciples; after that we are servants who proclaim the Gospel and celebrate the sacraments. We are searchers for Wisdom, teachers of the Faith, healers, and listeners. We share the joy of others, and also the sorrows. But first of all we are disciples.

Reflection: A View of the Life of the Priest

There is one fiddler painting of Chagall's that I like best. It is a village scene. Most people are in their houses. On the street is the fiddler. He is playing a tune and dancing along with it. Following him is a young man, a boy. He seems to be entranced by the fiddling. Is he attracted by the spectacle? Or, does he not understand? Or, is he just quite innocent? The painting has strong colours, expressing vibrancy and life. Clearly the fiddler brings something exciting to the village. Further back in the painting there is a couple standing outside their house. They are watching, but from a distance. In their posture there is hesitancy and apprehension. Unlike the young man they are aware that the fiddler represents something more than a music provider. They appreciate that he has a unique role within their small village community.

He helps them celebrate important events – happy ones and sad ones. At events rejoicing in the birth of a new member of the village family, he will lead them all in a cheerful song full of gratitude for the wonder of life. When people marry in the village he will lead them in stepping out in time to a dance of coming together, and also with variations on the theme of life he will set the time for them discovering the dance of life itself. The Spanish poet Federico García Lorca in his poem "The Guitar" describes guitar playing as a crying sound in the early hours of the morning: "there begins the cry of the guitar."[47] This is what Chagall is doing I think with his fiddler: as well as the happy events, the fiddler accompanies people through the difficult times. The fiddler may be a jovial fiddler, or a serious fiddler, but he cannot be a clown.

In the background of the painting, behind the vivacious colour, there is a darkness. It is this darkness which moves us to grasp an intensity in the painting, and in the lives of the villagers. The couple standing at their door know that there are hidden depths to this fiddler. And, this perturbs them. Behind his jocular exterior he is challenging them to discover a deeper understanding of life.

Yet the heavy colours of the painting also point to the darkness from which the fiddler's music comes. It is the darkness of God's presence. And, although it is dark, it is good. He is playing music which is more than mere tunes. He is inviting them to follow him to the place where the music is made. Or, as the poet Seamus Heaney says: "sing yourself to where the singing comes from."[48] Chagall's fiddler is enticing them to become the music itself. But this means letting go of many of the securities which other people say are important. So, they are uneasy, because they have a sense that what shapes the fiddler is the time when they do not see him, the time when he is on his own; they know that if they listened carefully to the fiddler when he is alone, they would hear little, or nothing, but they would feel that the music was playing in him, in an intense way, deep within his fragile humanity. This is something of the life of the priest – the priest with the parish community, the priest on his own, the priest standing before God.

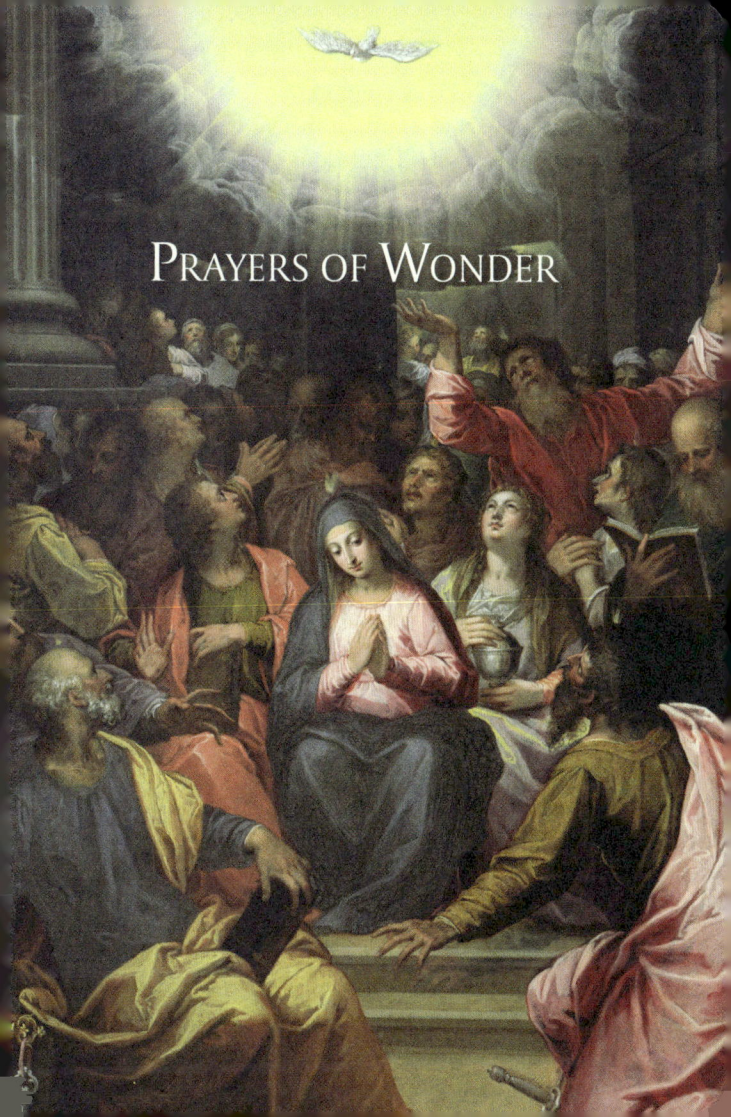

PRAYERS OF WONDER

The prayers in this collection were written during one of my summer visits to Taizé. In them I have tried to keep myself open to the wonder of God's presence, as well as the simple beauty which can be witnessed at Taizé.

Taizé is a small village in the Burgundy region of France. Situated at the edge of the village is a monastic community of monks called the Community of Taizé. The brothers of Taizé live a simple life committed to working for the reconciliation of Christians and of all peoples. Throughout the year people visit the community in order to join in its prayer. At the summer time this group of people is numbered in the thousands, and most of these are young people. One evening I listened to the simple, beautiful singing which filled the church in the praise of God. Then I wondered: was this volume of praise to God not also the voice of God whispering to us? Your words are spirit Lord and they are life.

Please use these prayers if they help you in your prayer. Start by reminding yourself that you are already in God's presence. A useful starting prayer is this:

> Lord Jesus,
> you are here,
> you are with us,
> you are in us.

Repeat it a few times. But remember that these prayers are designed to help you. All that you really need for prayer is to sit quietly and know that you are in God's presence.

Trust

Lord Jesus, I am going to trust you.
I am going to give my life over to you.
This does not mean that I won't worry –
of course I will,
I am an imperfect human being.
Sometimes people say: "Don't worry."
But that's easy if you're not the worrying type.
I do worry.
I worry about many things – some big, some small.
So, when people encourage me not to worry,
I give polite replies, but know I will worry.
You, I think, are not telling me not to worry,
because it is part of being human;
instead, you are asking me to trust you.
Compared to you, I know nothing;
so, even if I did not worry,
it would give me no more understanding of things.
Everything ordered by you is good –
it doesn't need to be understood by me.
Lord Jesus, I am going to trust you.

CREATION

Lord Jesus,
your creation is wonderful;
But so full was God's love
that God wanted to share it.
So, God created the Heavens and the Earth.
God created the mountains and the oceans.
God created plants and trees and flowers
    and animals.
Then God desired to make a part of Creation
that would be in God's image and likeness,
a part that could respond to that perfect love;
so, God created us – all of us.
The birds are singing in the trees;
the children are playing in the garden;
the young man takes his girlfriend's hand.
Lord Jesus, your creation is wonderful.
it is the glorious work of your hand.
Before the Earth existed,
before the plants and stars,
before any sort of universe,
what existed was God's love.

LEAVEN

Lord Jesus,
you ask us to be leaven
for the whole human family.
Just as the leaven helps
the bread to rise,
you ask us
to be like leaven in the world
raising up our sisters and brothers.
When we start doing this
we learn that our common union
becomes our nourishment.
But there is the possibility of more.
As your Spirit breathed into the bread
changes it into the Body of Christ,
so this same Spirit breathes in us,
bringing us into a human communion.
Then we might be the bread for the hungry
and strength for the weak.
Lord Jesus, you ask us to be leaven
for the whole human family.

SMALLNESS

Lord Jesus,
we are small.
The cosmos is big.
The universe is big.
Our solar system is big.
The sun is huge and hot
and warming and life-enhancing.
The moon is big
and in its quiet nocturnal way
comforting.
We are small.
Our world is big,
and although we live only
in a small part of it,
we allow the bigness
to confuse us sometimes.
There are times when our ideas are big
and we think fanciful things.
Lord Jesus, we are small,
and you love us in our smallness.

Sunshine

Lord Jesus,
I like the sunshine.
Of course I do.
Why would I not?
It keeps the world bright.
It helps the garden remain green.
It gives warmth.
But I like it for more than that.
I like it because you made it.
You made it so that we
might see each other clearly;
and, like the gardens, we too
might grow in your praise.
The sunshine helps us
to see clearly, but then
it asks us to look at each other
with a sense of the wonder
that can only come from you.
Lord Jesus,
I like the sunshine.

HOPE

Lord Jesus,
you are our hope –
not just the one who gives hope,
but hope itself.
Many of our brothers and sisters
live without a sense of hope.
They have become dulled
by being self-satisfied.
The hope you offer
keeps us moving forward to something better –
    that 'something better' is your life.
You are this hope itself –
you take us to yourself.
Even if we feel empty
you help us to be filled by goodness.
Take my hand.
Take me with you
to the fullness of your life.
Lord Jesus,
you are our hope.

Gentleness

Lord Jesus,
you come to us in gentleness.
You say to us:
"I am gentle and humble of heart."
You ask us to be gentle
with each other.
This gentleness is softness;
it is care;
it is understanding;
but it is not weakness.
You say to us:
"Come to me, all you who labour
and are overburdened."
You give us rest because
you are gentle and humble of heart.
Give us the strength to be gentle.
Give us the courage
to carry each other's burdens.
Lord Jesus,
you come to us in gentleness.

OPENNESS

Lord Jesus,
teach us to be open.
One of the beautiful things
I have learnt
is the need for the Church,
all of us who are baptised,
to be open to the Spirit and the world.
I don't mean open to anything.
I mean to be open to the ways
in which the whole world
might learn the ways
of the Holy Spirit,
and learn through us, the Church.
We, therefore, need to be open –
open to the Spirit of God;
open to God's wonders;
open to God's simplicity;
open to God's presence.
Lord Jesus,
teach us to be open.

JOY

Lord Jesus,
you are our joy.
You are the joy that fills us.
This joy invites us to find
in ourselves and in others
a life that is so simple,
so good,
so beautiful,
so true.
Finding it requires that
we give ourselves over to you.
It is not a product
to be bought;
it is not an achievement.
It is the deep down trust
of the simple-hearted.
It is an uncomplicated
celebration of your life in us.
Lord Jesus,
you are our joy.

Reconciliation

Lord Jesus,
you call us to reconciliation.
This is not easy.
Where is this reconciliation to be?
It ought to be a serious attempt
between Christians;
reconciliation between different religions;
reconciliation between those who have hurt
and those who have been hurt;
reconciliation between our true selves
and our false selves.
But this demands a great deal.
It challenges us to look
beyond the boundaries of our own world –
to see where we live
as the door into your kingdom.
Then we will see each other as citizens
of heaven, helping each other on the way.
Lord Jesus,
you call us to reconciliation.

Rain

Lord Jesus,
thank you for the rain.
It falls so effortlessly,
without cost, or complaint,
or any such thing.
We can talk about cloud formation,
or molecules, or air pressure;
it is simpler than that –
the rain is your gift to us.
It is not like a birthday gift,
or a Christmas gift,
but one of those we give
just to show our love.
In giving such a gift,
we bring each other to new life.
The rain is your gift
to renew your life within us.
It is life; it is love.
Lord Jesus,
thank you for the rain.

BEAUTY

Lord Jesus,
your beauty surrounds us.
We see it in the wonder
of your creation –
it is a reflection of your goodness.
We see it in the care of parents –
it is God the Father's care for us.
We see it in husbands and wives –
their commitment to each other,
is a sign of your commitment to us.
We see your beauty
in life that is fragile –
please look after it, Lord.
We see it in the brokenness of life –
please heal it, Lord.
Your beauty, Lord,
shines out
from the deepest part of ourselves.
Lord Jesus,
Your beauty surrounds us.

BREATH OF GOD

Lord Jesus,
send the Breath of God
into our lives –
to enliven us,
to comfort us,
to encourage us,
to renew and revitalise your Church.
Breathe into us
the life of the resurrection,
so that even now we will be
living the life of heaven.
Breathe your life
into every part of us –
our bodies,
our minds,
our memories,
our relations with each other.
Lord Jesus,
send the Breath of God
into our lives.

GENEROSITY

Lord Jesus,
you teach us generosity.
Often we use this word
to describe some small act
of giving money.
You teach us that generosity
is about giving ourselves.
It demands that we give
our time and understanding
to others.
It demands preferring others
to ourselves.
It demands that we respect
the views of others
when they differ from ours;
that we respond with humility
to the views of others
when they need correction.
Lord Jesus,
you teach us generosity.

Risen Christ

Lord Jesus,
you are the Risen Christ.
You are the one who overcame death
in your glorious resurrection.
You subjected yourself
to the consequences of our sin,
so that in dying and rising
you might free us.
And, in your moment of death
you entered into a cosmic battle;
it was one which the powers of evil
were always going to lose,
for you are the Lord of Life.
Death could hold no sway
over you.
Your rising is still today.
You rise in us,
bringing us to life.
Lord Jesus,
you are the Risen Christ.

Peace

Lord Jesus,
peace is your gift to us.
But it is more
than words said at Mass.
It is an invitation
to relate to each other
according to what builds unity –
unity between peoples;
unity between the different parts
of our own lives.
When we find this peace
we rejoice in being alive,
in celebrating different cultures
and languages and customs,
in knowing that we are one family.
Help us search for your peace,
to find your peace
and to live it with others.
Lord Jesus,
peace is your gift to us.

Image and Likeness

Lord Jesus,
you reveal yourself to us
in all your people.
I see lots of people –
some I know,
most I don't.
Some profess you as Lord;
others do that in different ways.
Many say they don't believe
in God at all.
Yet, Lord, you reveal yourself
in all of them.
What's so wonderful
is that everyone is unique –
no two are the same.
And, every unique person
reveals you to the world.
Lord Jesus,
you reveal yourself to us
in all your people.

LIFE

Lord Jesus,
you are our life.
You said:
"I am the way, the truth and the life."
Often we focus on "the truth"
and then get caught up
in clever debates
about what is right.
You are our life.
Help us to enjoy
living with you;
to enjoy being alive with you;
to feel the excitement
of your presence,
and the consolation
of your apparent absence.
May your life be
a wellspring inside us.
Lord Jesus,
you are our life.

Mercy

Lord Jesus,
you show us your mercy.
When we offend you,
in any way, and deserve
the exercise of your justice,
you go beyond justice,
and show us your mercy.
When we wrong you
or others
(which is also wronging you)
justice is what we deserve.
But time and again
you offer us mercy –
mercy is something
we can never deserve,
it is always your free gift.
And, the gift asks us
to share it with others.
Lord Jesus,
you show us your mercy.

Love

Lord Jesus,
I love you.
With every movement of my body,
every passing thought,
every hope and aspiration,
every memory,
I love you.
With every beat of my heart,
I know that it's love
of you,
that makes me live.
And, even when it's not easy,
Even then do I love you.
I love you in the morning,
and during the day,
and in the evening,
and during the night hours,
and in the morning again.
Lord Jesus,
I love you.

Endnotes

1 Thomas Merton, *Thomas Merton on Saint Bernard* (Kalamazoo: Cistercian Publications, 1980) p. 28.

2 Jean Vanier, *Community and Growth* (New York: Paulist Press, 1979, 2nd rev. ed. 1989) p. 108.

3 St John of the Cross, "The Dark Night", in *The Collected Works of St John of the Cross*, (trans. Kieran Kavanagh, OCD and Otilio Rodriguez, OCD) (Washington: ICS Publications, 1979) p. 712.

4 Jean Vanier, *Signs of the Times* (London: DLT, 2013) p. 107.

5 Jean Lebon, *How to Understand the Liturgy* (London: SCM Press Ltd, 1987) p. 18.

6 Henri Nouwen, *Clowning in Rome, Reflections on Solitude, Celibacy, Prayer and Contemplation* (Garden City, New York: Image Books, 1979) p. 54.

7 Brother Roger of Taizé, *The Rule of Taizé in French and English* (London: SPCK, 2012) p. 59.

8 St John of the Cross, "Cántico Espiritual", in *The Collected Works of St John of the Cross*, (trans. Kieran Kavanagh, OCD and Otilio Rodriguez, OCD) (Washington: ICS Publications, 1979) p. 714 (trans. G. Bogan, 2017).

9 St Paul VI, *Mysterium Fidei* (London: CTS, 1965) ch. 35.

10 William T. Ditewig, *The Emerging Diaconate, Servant Leaders in a Servant Church* (Mahwah, New Jersey: Paulist Press, 2007) p. 219.

11 E.H. Gombrich, *The Story of Art* (London: Phaidon Press, 2006, pocket edition) p. 129.

12 Pope Francis, *Evangelii Gaudium* (London: CTS, 2013) ch. 124.

13 Daniel Rees, et al., *Consider Your Call, A Theology of Monastic Life Today* (London: SPCK, 1978) pp. 243-4.

14 *Declaration on the Relation of the Church to Non-Christian Religions* (London: CTS, 1966) ch. 1.

15 Brother Roger of Taizé, *The Rule of Taizé in French and English* (London: SPCK, 2012) p. 47.

16 George Mackay Brown, *For the Islands I Sing* (Edinburgh: Polygon, 2008) p. 174.

17 Hans Urs von Balthasar, *Prayer* (London: Geoffrey Chapman, 1961) p. 32.

18 Jean Vanier, *Community and Growth* (New York: Paulist Press, 1979, 2nd rev. ed. 1989) p. 253.

19 Rowan Williams, *Being Disciples* (Grand Rapids: Eerdmans Publishing Co, 2016) p. 18.

20 "Pangur Bán", (trans.) Robin Flower, in (eds) Seamus Heaney and Ted Hughes, *The School Bag* (London: Faber and Faber, 1997) pp. 224-5.

21 Edward Schillebeeckx, *Jesus in our Western Culture, Mysticism, Ethics and Politics* (London: SCM Press Ltd, 1987) p. 70.

22 Thomas Merton, *The Life of the Vows, Initiation into the Monastic Tradition 6* (ed.) Patrick F O'Connell (Collegeville: Liturgical Press and Cistercian Publications, 2012) pp. 241-2.

23 Pope Francis, *Evangelii Gaudium* (London: CTS, 2013) ch. 47.

24 T.S. Eliot, *Murder in the Cathedral* (London: Faber and Faber, 1965).

25 Congregation for the Clergy, *Directory on the Ministry and Life of Priests* (London: CTS, 1996) ch. 30.

26 Karl Rahner, *Servants of the Lord* (London: Burns and Oates, 1968) p. 68.

27 Pope John Paul II, *Gift and Mystery* (London: CTS, 1997) p. 22.

28 Robert W.K.C. Rogerson, *Jack Coia: His Life and Work* (Glasgow: Robert W.K.C. Rogerson, 1986) p. 102.

29 Donald McGlynn, *Atlas Martyrs, Vol. 1*, http://nunraw.blogspot.co.uk/2011/12/atlas-martyrs-vol-1.html, accessed 2nd May 2017.

30 St Paul VI, *Evangelii Nuntiandi* (London: CTS, 1996) ch. 41.

31 "En la Comunidad Todos Deben dar Testimonio Profético, no Sólo Algunos," Leonardo Boff, *Eclesiogénesis: las Comunidades de Base Reinventan la Iglesia* (Santander: Sal Terrae, 1979) p. 41.

32 Gustavo Gutiérrez, *A Theology of Liberation* (London: SCM Press Ltd, 1974, rev. ed. 1988) p. 148.

33   St Teresa of Avila, (trans.) Kieran Kavanaugh, OCD and Otilio Rodriguez, OCD, *The Collected Works of St Teresa of Avila, Vol. 2* (Washington, DC: ICS Publications, 1980) ch. 30.7.

34   Pope St John Paul II, *Novo Millennio Ineunte* (London: CTS, Epiphany 2001) n. 33.

35   Karol Wojtyla, *Sign of Contradiction* (Slough: St Paul Publications, 1979) pp. 131-2.

36   William Shakespeare, *Measure for Measure*, V.1.

37   Joseph Ratzinger, *Called to Communion, Understanding the Church Today* (San Francisco: Ignatius Press, 1996) p. 128.

38   Aristotle, (trans.) Ernest Baker, *The Politics* (Oxford: OUP, 1995) n.1253ª25, p. 11.

39   Brother Roger of Taizé, *The Rule of Taizé in French and English* (London: SPCK, 2012) p. 61.

40   Daniel Rees, et al., *Consider Your Call, A Theology of Monastic Life Today* (London: SPCK, 1978) p. 138.

41   R.S. Thomas, "The Country Clergy" in *Collected Poems, 1945-1990* (London: Phoenix Press, 2001) p. 82.

42   Donald McGlynn, *Atlas Martyrs, Vol. 1*, http://nunraw.blogspot.co.uk/2011/12/atlas-martyrs-vol-1.html, accessed 2nd May 2017.

43   John J. Haldane, "The Need of Spirituality in Catholic Education" in (ed.) James C Conroy, *Catholic Education Inside-Out/Outside-In* (Dublin: Lindisfarne Books, 1999) pp. 188-206.

44   Henri Nouwen, *Bread for the Journey, Reflections for Every Day of the Year* (London: DLT, 1996) p. 244.

45   Congregation for the Clergy, *Directory on the Ministry and Life of Priests* (London: CTS, 1996) ch. 70, 73.

46   Mother Teresa of Calcutta and Brother Roger of Taizé, *Mary, Mother of Reconciliations* (London: Mowbray, 1987, repr. 1989) p. 43.

47   Federico García Lorca, "La guitarra", in *Selected Poems* (London: Penguin Books, 1997) p. 27 (trans. G. Bogan).

48   Seamus Heaney, "At the Wellhead", in *The Spirit Level* (London: Faber and Faber, 1996) p. 65.